ZOOLOGY QUIZ

Edited by

GEORGE BROWN

ANMOL PUBLICATIONS PVT. LTD.
NEW DELHI-110002 (INDIA)

ANMOL PUBLICATIONS PVT. LTD.
4374/4B, Ansari Road, Daryaganj
New Delhi-110 002

Zoology Quiz

First Edition 1994
Reprint 1996, 1997, 1998
Reprint 1999
ISBN 81-7041-898-4

PRINTED IN INDIA

Published by J. L. Kumar for Anmol Publications Pvt. Ltd., New Delhi-110 002 and Printed at Mehra Offset Press, Delhi.

Preface

Quiz series on Physics, Chemistry, Science, Mathematics, Botany and Zoology, has been written, compiled and edited by the experts of their respective fields. The purpose of the series is to enable students to assess their knowledge and understanding of the subject concerned. Each book includes more than 1000 questions. Every question included in this series has been extensively tested with school as well as college students. By means of these questions one can test not only factual recall but any other qualities that seem desirable, e.g., powers of deduction, ability to weigh evidence, apply known principles to new situations etc. Questions may be either factual or may involve a fair amount of reasoning before a decision can be made.

The Editor

Directions: *Each of the following questions is followed by for responses (answers). Select the correct response in each case. Show your answer by putting a cross against the response.*

Section I

Q. 1. A food substance made up of carbohydrates was acted upon by digestive enzymes, and the products were tested by heating with Benedict's solution. Which of the following results indicates that the food substance has been fully hydrolysed:

(*a*) a dark blue precipitate was formed.
(*b*) the food substance gave a yellow precipitate.
(*c*) the food substance with the Benedict's solution gave a brick red precipitate
(*d*) the food substance reacted with the Benedict's solution and gave a brown precipitate.

Q. 2. The presence of *Entamoeba histolytica* in public water is a sign of:

(*a*) Clean water.
(*b*) Polluted water
(*c*) Bacteria outbreak.
(*d*) Decay.

Q. 3. The mammalian vertebrae are differentiated into the cervical, thoracic, lumbar and caudal vertebrae. Which of the following statements is not true of a cervical vertebra.

(*a*) flattened transverse processes
(*b*) presence of short neural spine
(*c*) presence of vertebraterial canal
(*d*) presence of a stout centrum.

Q. 4. The mammalian heart receives oxygenated blood from

(*a*) anterior vena cava
(*b*) pulmonary artery
(*c*) pulmonary vein
(*d*) the dorsal aorta.

Q. 5. The lungs are the sites of oxygen uptake into the tissues. The oxygen is used to

(*a*) oxidise food substances
(*b*) release energy to the tissues
(*c*) prevent anaerobic respiration
(*d*) ensure release on energy CO_2 and H_2O.

Q. 6. The maintenance of a uniform internal environment in a mammal is due to

(*a*) loss of water by the sweet glands
(*b*) loss of metabolites by the kidney
(*c*) regulatory actions of the kidney, sweat glands and lungs
(*d*) uptake of water through the mouth.

Q. 7. A man working in a science laboratory, accidentially inserted his hand into concentrated sulphuric acid solution. He was able to feel a burning sensation because

(*a*) his skin a sensitive
(*b*) his skin contains sensory and motor cells
(*c*) his skin receptor cells conveyed the impulse to the spiral cord for interpretation
(*d*) the sensory cells passed the impulse to the motor cells.

Q. 8. Which of the following statements about intestinal worm is inaccurate?

(*a*) Intestinal worms are parasitic
(*b*) Intestinal worms usually have secondary hosts
(*c*) Intestinal worms produce a large number of offspring in their hosts
(*d*) Intestinal worms derive their food from their host.

Q. 9. Mineral or vitamin deficiency is accompanied by various symptoms. Which of the following statements is correct?

(*a*) Calcium deficiency results in bad sight
(*b*) Iron deficiency leads to loss of blood
(*c*) Ascorbic acid deficiency causes anaemia
(*d*) Vitamin B, deficiency leads to scurvy.

Q. 10. In a lake, the stability of life of the inhabitants depends on

(*a*) the aquatic fishes and reptiles
(*b*) the phytoplankton, algae and other aquatic plants
(*c*) the zooplankton and other micro-organisms
(*d*) the activities of the micro-organisms and the fishes.

Q. 11. A student suffering from short sightedness can have this fault corrected by wearing a spectacle fitted with

(*a*) double convex lense
(*b*) single concave lense
(*c*) double concave lense
(*d*) refractive lense.

Q. 12. The mammalian fore limb is made of

(*a*) humerus, ulna, radius, tarsals, phalanges
(*b*) humerus, tibia, fibula, tarsals, phalanges
(*c*) humerus, ulna, radius, carpals, phalanges
(*d*) humerus, ulna, fibula, carpals, phalanges.

Q. 13. The life history of insects includes either complete or incomplete metamorphosis. Which of the following sequence is true of complete metamorphosis?

(*a*) Egg, larva, nymph, imago
(*b*) Egg, larva, pupa, imago
(*c*) Egg, nymph, imago
(*d*) Egg, larva, imago.

Q. 14. A rat embryo derives its nutrition from the parent

(*a*) by sucking
(*b*) by making contact with mother's blood vessels
(*c*) through the placenta
(*d*) by direct diffusion through the blood vessels in the uterus.

Q. 15. You are confronted with a lion. Which of these hormones will be released into your blood stream

(*a*) Insulin
(*b*) Gastrin
(*c*) Thyroxine
(*d*) Adrenaline.

Q. 16. Which of these is the function of the Eustachian tube?

(*a*) An exit for the dirt in the middle ear
(*b*) Transmission of sound from the mouth to the tympanic membrane
(*c*) Reception of sound stimulus
(*d*) Equalizing the pressure of the air in the middle ear with that outside.

Q. 17. A boy who cannot see distant objects is said to have a defect called

(*a*) astigmatism
(*b*) cataract of the eye
(*c*) hypermetropia
(*d*) myopia

Q. 18. The small gap occuring between 2 axons is called

(*a*) nodes of ranvier
(*b*) dendrites
(*c*) synapse
(*d*) nerve bridges.

Q. 19. The main excretory organ in insects is

(*a*) malpighian tubules
(*b*) hepatic caeca
(*c*) hind gut
(*d*) uriniferous tubules.

Q. 20. Excretion can be defined as

(*a*) elimination of urea from the body
(*b*) passing out of excreta
(*c*) elimination of poisonous by-products of metabolism
(*d*) deamination of amino acids to form urea.

Q. 21. Which of these is not characteristic of amphibians.

(*a*) They lay their eggs in water
(*b*) They have diaphragm
(*c*) They respire by means of the skin
(*d*) They have smooth glandular skin.

(*a*) to aerate the soil
(*b*) to keep water in the soil
(*c*) replenish the organic content of the soil
(*d*) to break down large particles of soil.

Q. 23. When a biologist describes an animal as 'warm-blooded', he means that its

(*a*) Skin prevents loss or gain of heat
(*b*) The kidneys remove heat from the blood
(*c*) Temperature is lower in the cold season than in the hot season
(*d*) Temperature tends to remain constant at most times.

Q. 24. Which of the following procedures would you select to determine whether or not a certain animal is an insect?

(*a*) Count the number of legs
(*b*) Count the number of wings
(*c*) Make sure that the specimen has only two body segments
(*d*) Make sure that the specimen has antennae.

Q. 25. For proper development of bones, children's diets must be rich in CALCIUM,

(*a*) Phosphorus and Iron
(*b*) Iron and Vitamin D
(*c*) Vitamin D and Iodine
(*d*) Phosphorus and Vitamin D.

Q. 26. Which of the following nutrients would you NOT expect to find in the capillaries of the intestinal villus?

(*a*) Sucrose
(*b*) Glucose
(*c*) Amino-acids
(*d*) Galactose.

Q. 27. A patient whose gall-bladder is removed will experience difficulty in digesting fat because he will no longer.

(*a*) Secrete insulin
(*b*) Produce lipase
(*c*) Secrete renin
(*d*) Store bile.

Q. 28. The tricuspid valve lies between the

(*a*) left auricle and left ventricle
(*b*) right auricle and right ventricle
(*c*) right ventricle and pulmonary artery
(*d*) left ventricle and aorta.

Q. 29. In the respiration of a fish, the oxygen is absorbed through

(*a*) gill arch
(*b*) gill raker
(*c*) gill cover
(*d*) gill filament.

Q. 30. The removal of waste food from the intestine is called:

(*a*) Assimilation
(*b*) Excretion
(*c*) Defaecation
(*d*) Digestion.

Q. 31. Which of the following skin structures are thought to be the ones modified to form mammary glands?

(*a*) Hair follicles
(*b*) Hair papilla
(*c*) Sebaceous glands
(*d*) Malpighian layer.

Q. 32. Blood vessels whose walls are best adapted for diffusion of substances are:

(*a*) Capillaries
(*b*) Arteries
(*c*) Veins
(*d*) Lacteals.

Q. 33. The part of the brain where conscious thought occurs is

(*a*) Olfactory lobe
(*b*) Cerebrum
(*c*) Cerebellum
(*d*) Medula oblongata.

Q. 34. The part of the nerve cell that carries impulses to the main body of the nerve-cell is the

(*a*) Neurilemma
(*b*) Axon
(*c*) Dendrite
(*d*) Nucleus.

Following is the simplified picture of the carbon cycle, study it carefully and answer questions 35 and 36

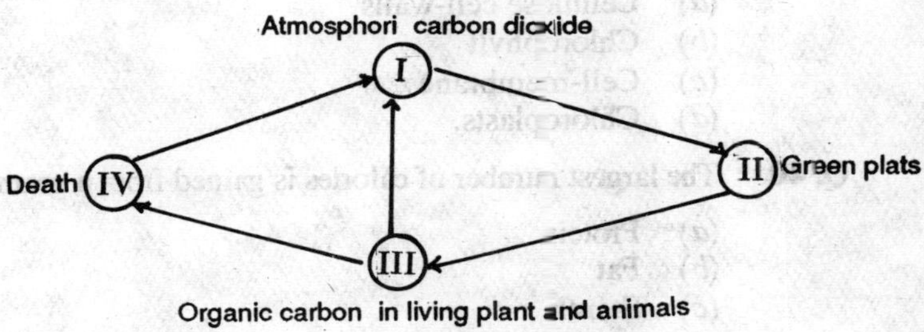

Q. 35. What is the name of the process indicated by the arrow between III and I?

(*a*) Photosynthesis
(*b*) Respiration
(*c*) Decay
(*d*) Excretion.

Q. 36. Energy enters the system at the point between

(*a*) I and II
(*b*) II and III
(*c*) III and IV
(*d*) IV and I.

Q. 37. Which of the following statements best defines sexual reproduction?

(*a*) Male and female parents mate
(*b*) Two parents co-operate in the process
(*c*) Offspring arises from the fusion of two special cells
(*d*) Sperms are generally small and motile.

Q. 38. A vertebrate that can breathe under water is the

(*a*) Whale
(*b*) Crocodile
(*c*) Water turtle
(*d*) Tilapia.

Q. 39. Which of the following structures is MOST commonly found in plant cells but NOT in animal cells?

(*a*) Cellulose cell-walls
(*b*) Chlorophyll
(*c*) Cell-membrane
(*d*) Chloroplasts.

Q. 40. The largest number of calories is gained from a gramme of

(*a*) Protein
(*b*) Fat
(*c*) Starch
(*d*) Sugar.

Q. 41. A nutrient with the chemical formula $C_{12}H_{12}O_{11}$ is likely to be

(*a*) Fructose
(*b*) Sucrose
(*c*) Protein
(*d*) Amino acid.

Q. 42. Which of the following is NOT a proper food-chain?

(*a*) Man-termites-wood
(*b*) Tiger-man-pig-root
(*c*) Man-fish-meat-plant juices
(*d*) Hawk-chicken-seeds.

Q. 43. Usually, in most food-chains, the

(*a*) plant-eaters outnumber the plants
(*b*) plant-eaters outnumber the flesh-eaters
(*c*) flesh-eaters outnumber the plant-eaters
(*d*) flesh-eaters outnumber the plants.

Q. 44. Excretion means

(*a*) Sweating

(*b*) Defaecation
(*c*) Getting rid of waste metabolic by-products
(*d*) Removing excess water from the body.

Q. 45. The material from which cells of living organism are made is called

(*a*) Colloid
(*b*) Nucleoplasm
(*c*) Cytoplasm
(*d*) Protoplasm.

Q. 46. Water is absorbed through the root-hairs by means of

(*a*) Respiration
(*b*) Tugor pressure
(*c*) Transpiration
(*d*) Osmosis.

Q. 47. Which of these transmits malaria parasites to man

(*a*) Culex
(*b*) Housefly
(*c*) Anopheles
(*d*) Aedes.

Q. 48. Dysentry is caused by

(*a*) Eating food containing excess sugar
(*b*) Protozoan parasite called Entamoeba histolytica
(*c*) Plasmodium
(*d*) Malnutrition.

Q. 49. The organism involved in the conversion of nitrogen to nitrates in the nodules of certain plants are called

(*a*) Bacteria
(*b*) Fungi
(*c*) Termites
(*d*) Worms.

Q. 50. Neurons are most highly specialised for

(*a*) Contractibility
(*b*) Conduction
(*c*) Responsiveness
(*d*) Secretion.

Q. 51. The common feature of the skin, kidney and the lungs in a mammals is

(*a*) Loss of water
(*b*) Reabsorption of glucose
(*c*) Removal of nitrogenous waste from the body
(*d*) Manufacture of vitamin D in sunlight.

Q. 52. Oxygenated blood from the lungs is brought by the pulmonary veins to the

(*a*) Right auricle
(*b*) Left auricle
(*c*) Right ventricle
(*d*) Left ventricle.

Q. 53. Irritability means

(*a*) Ability to respond to stimuli
(*b*) Positive response to light
(*c*) Movement due to touch
(*d*) Response to chemicals in the environment.

Q. 54. The system involved in food transport in plant and animal tissues is known as the

(*a*) Circulatory system
(*b*) Transpiration system
(*c*) Vascular system
(*d*) Vascular bundle.

Q. 55. The breaking down of simple sugar to alcohol, carbon dioxide and energy is called

(*a*) Respiration
(*b*) Oxidation
(*c*) Fermentation
(*d*) Digestion.

Q. 56. If a mosquito larva eats diatoms and the larva is in turn eaten by a fish and the fish is eaten by a bird, the association could be described as

(*a*) Commensalism
(*b*) Parasitism

(*c*) Saprophytism
(*d*) Food chain.

Q. 57. Which of the following does not contain a nucleus when matured?

(*a*) A mammalian red blood cell
(*b*) A root hair
(*c*) A pollen grain
(*d*) An ovum.

Q. 58. Which of the following substances is manufactured by the liver?

(*a*) Pepsin
(*b*) Renin
(*c*) Bile
(*d*) Insulin.

Q. 59. The Housefly breathes by means of

(*a*) Gills
(*b*) Lungs
(*c*) Air sacs
(*d*) Tracheal tubes.

Q. 60. Which one of the following combinations most completely expresses the products of oxidation of a carbohydrate?

(*a*) Carbon dioxide, urea, mineral salts
(*b*) Energy, mineral salts, carbon dioxide
(*c*) Energy water, carbon dioxide
(*d*) Glucose, energy, urea.

Q. 61. A typical lumbar does not have a

(*a*) Neural arch
(*b*) Neural spine
(*c*) Neural canal
(*d*) Vertebrarterial canal.

Q. 62. The function of the neural canal in the vertebrae is to

(*a*) Protect the spinal cord
(*b*) Provide attachment of muscles
(*c*) Support the weight of the visceral
(*d*) Allow for bending and twisting.

Q. 63. What is the name given to the outer, clear part of the protoplasm of Amoeba?

(*a*) Endoplasm
(*b*) Cytoplasm
(*c*) Ectoplasm
(*d*) Endoderm.

Q. 64. The flesh eating animals are

(*a*) Arthropoda
(*b*) Vegetarians
(*c*) Carnivora
(*d*) Rodentia.

Q. 65. Black rat is an example of

(*a*) A herbivorous animal
(*b*) A carnivorous animal
(*c*) An omnivorous animal
(*d*) A parasitic animal.

Q. 66. The largest gland in mammal is

(*a*) Pancreas
(*b*) Spleen
(*c*) Thyroid
(*d*) Liver.

Q. 67. Which is an invertebrate?

(*a*) Rat
(*b*) Tilapia
(*c*) Toad
(*d*) Mosquito larva.

Q. 68. Which of the following is a human digestive enzyme which functions best in an acid medium?

(*a*) Insulin
(*b*) Pepsin
(*c*) An intestinal enzyme
(*d*) Ptyalin.

Q. 69. Which of the following contains all of the elements, hydrogen, oxygen and nitrogen?

(*a*) Sugar
(*b*) Fat
(*c*) Starch
(*d*) Protein.

Q. 70. Which of these vertebrae has an odontoid peg?

(*a*) Axis
(*b*) Lumbar
(*c*) Atlas
(*d*) Thoracic.

Q. 71. In complete darkness the pupils of the eyes are

(*a*) Small
(*b*) Large
(*c*) White in colour
(*d*) Can not change.

Q. 72. Which of these is characteristic of mammals?

(*a*) Possession of feathers
(*b*) Possession of dry skin
(*c*) Possession of cold body
(*d*) Possession of hairs.

Q. 73. A tse-tse fly carries the germs which cause

(*a*) Malaria
(*b*) Sleeping sickness
(*c*) Elephantiasis
(*d*) Headache.

Q. 74. Parasitism means

(*a*) Living together with or without advantage
(*b*) Living together for mutual benefit
(*c*) An association between two organisms in which one gains and other loses.
(*d*) An association between a plant and animal.

Q. 75. Which explains complete metamorphosis?

(*a*) Egg, larva, adult
(*b*) Larva, pupal, adult
(*c*) Adult, egg, pupal
(*d*) Egg, larva, pupal, adult.

Q. 76. Which of these insects is beneficial to man

(*a*) Housefly
(*b*) Mosquito
(*c*) Beetle
(*d*) Honey bee.

Q. 77. Which of these is a Protozoan?

(*a*) Paramecium
(*b*) Spider
(*c*) Termite
(*d*) Earthworm.

Q. 78. Fish can survive in water because

(*a*) It is a vertebrate
(*b*) The body is stream-lined
(*c*) Respiration is by gill
(*d*) It has a tail.

Q. 79. The main function of protein to animal is

(*a*) as a food reserve
(*b*) to build up the tissues
(*c*) to form urea
(*d*) to make the blood cells healthy.

Q. 80. Short-sightedness may be corrected by

(*a*) Using spectacles with convex lenses
(*b*) Eating food rich in vitamin A
(*c*) Using spectacles with coloured lenses
(*d*) Using spectacles with concave lenses.

Q. 81. Urine is carried from the bladder by

(*a*) Fallopian tube
(*b*) Ureter
(*c*) Urethra
(*d*) Vagina.

Q. 82. Which part of the brain is concerned with learning?

(*a*) Pineal body
(*b*) Optic lobe
(*c*) Olfactory lobe
(*d*) Cerebral hemisphere.

Q. 83. Which is the correct test for reducing sugar?

(*a*) Sugar+Fehling solutions A and B
(*b*) Sugar+Concentrated nitric acid and boiled
(*c*) Sugar+Fehling solutions A and B and boiled
(*d*) Sugar+dilute sulphuric acid and boiled.

Q. 84. Which is not true of mammals?

(*a*) Possession of four chambered heart
(*b*) Complete double circulation
(*c*) Possession of different types of teeth
(*d*) Possession of exoskeleton.

Q. 85. Testosterone is produced in the

(*a*) Ovary
(*b*) Liver
(*c*) Testis
(*d*) Pancreas.

Q. 86. Which of these animals shows radial symmetry?

(*a*) Dog
(*b*) Hydra
(*c*) Amoeba
(*d*) Cockroach.

Q. 87. Which of these animals has no symmetry?

(*a*) Frog
(*b*) Snake
(*c*) Earthworm
(*d*) Amoeba.

Q. 88. Euglena is regarded as

(*a*) A plant only
(*b*) As animal only
(*c*) A saprophyte
(*d*) Intermediate between an animal and a plant.

Q. 89. Which is not a product of organic evolution?

(*a*) Man
(*b*) Rat

(*c*) Housefly
(*d*) Stone.

Q. 90. Which of the following is a sense organ.

(*a*) Skull
(*b*) Femur
(*c*) Ear
(*d*) Blood.

Q. 91. Chromosomes are located in the

(*a*) Cytoplasm
(*b*) Ectoplasm
(*c*) Endoplasm
(*d*) Nucleus.

Q. 92. Syphilis is a venereal disease caused by

(*a*) Treponema pallidum
(*b*) Neisseria gonorrhoeae
(*c*) Hemoephilus ducreyi
(*d*) Treponema pertenue.

Q. 93. When a hybrid black pig is crossed with a white pig, the offspring are

(*a*) Black
(*b*) White
(*c*) Some black and some white
(*d*) Some pure black.

Q. 94. If three quarters of the offspring of many experimental crosses show the dorminant character, the parents were

(*a*) Both pure dorminant
(*b*) Both pure recessive
(*c*) One dorminant, one recessive
(*d*) Both hybrid.

Q. 95. In the human body a cell that nearly resembles a one-called animal is

(*a*) Muscle cell
(*b*) Red blood cell
(*c*) White blood cell
(*d*) Nerve cell.

Q. 96. Animals without backbone are called

(*a*) Chordates
(*b*) Veretebrates
(*c*) Amphibians
(*d*) Invertebrates.

Q. 97. Spider belongs to the class

(*a*) Insecta
(*b*) Arachnida
(*c*) Myriapoda
(*d*) Crustacea.

Q. 98. Ecology is the study of animals and plants in relation to their

(*a*) Food
(*b*) Environment
(*c*) Temperature
(*d*) Reproduction.

Q. 99. The part of the cell which initiates cell division is called

(*a*) Cytoplasm
(*b*) Nucleus
(*c*) Vacuole
(*d*) Endoplasm.

Q. 100. The inability of the body to regulate the amount of glucose in the body may be due to

(*a*) Over activity of the kidneys
(*b*) The eating of a great amount of sugar
(*c*) The failure of the pancreas to produce insulin
(*d*) Inefficient respiration in the body.

Section II

Q. 101. Basically lymph is made up of

(*a*) Red and white corpuscles
(*b*) Venules and arterioles
(*c*) Blood plasma, red corpuscles and fats
(*d*) Blood plasma and some organic matter.

Q. 102. Which of the following does not limit the population of organisms?

(*a*) Length of day
(*b*) Migration
(*c*) Competition
(*d*) Number of offspring produced.

Q. 103. Hardplate is found in

(*a*) Domestic fowl
(*b*) Toad
(*c*) Beetle
(*d*) Honey bee.

Q. 104. A lipase catalyzes reactions involving

(*a*) polysaccharides
(*b*) nucleic acids
(*c*) proteins
(*d*) fats.

Q. 105. A cell will swell if the external medium is

(*a*) hypotonic
(*b*) hypertonic
(*c*) isotonic
(*d*) more concentrated than the protoplasm of the cell.

Q. 106. Osmosis involves

(*a*) diffusion of suspended particles from higher to lower concentration
(*b*) diffusion of suspended particles from lower to higher concentration
(*c*) diffusion of water from the more to the less concentrated side
(*d*) diffusion of water from the less to the more concentrated side.

Q. 107. An example of a tetrapyrrol pigment is

(*a*) carotene
(*b*) cytochrome
(*c*) xanthophyll
(*d*) melanin.

Q. 108. Permeability is

(*a*) the ability of a substance to cause osmosis
(*b*) the ability of a membrane to allow substances to pass through
(*c*) the loss of dissolved particles
(*d*) the loss of water.

Q. 109. The control center for the activities of the cell is the

(*a*) nucleus
(*b*) contractile vacuole
(*c*) mitochondria
(*d*) cell wall.

Q. 110. According to the Watson-Crick model, only one of the following is a possible purine-pyrimidine pair:

(*a*) adenine-guanine
(*b*) adenine-thymine
(*c*) adenine-cytosine
(*d*) adenine-uracil.

Q. 111. The specificity of DNA resides is

(*a*) the sequence of the phosphate-sugar components
(*b*) its protein
(*c*) the sequence of the purine-pyrimidine components
(*d*) the number of the nucleotide components.

Q. 112. Pelagic communities of the ocean are found

(*a*) in the open sea and not at the bottom
(*b*) at the margin of the sea on the bottom
(*c*) at great depths of the sea and on the bottom
(*d*) in none of the above locations.

Q. 113. Commensalism involves a relationship where

(*a*) an organism feeds on the tissues and organs of another living organism
(*b*) the host neither benefits nor is harmed by the presence of the guest
(*c*) an organism obtains its food from the dead bodies of other organisms
(*d*) both host and guest benefit from the presence of the other.

Q. 114. An inclusive natural habitat of wide geographic range that is made up of characteristic fauna and flora is the

(*a*) environment
(*b*) zone
(*c*) community
(*d*) biome.

Q. 115. The number of animals which are indirectly dependent on plants for food is

(*a*) greater than
(*b*) less than
(*c*) same as the number of animals directly dependent on plants for food
(*d*) None of these.

Q. 116. Some phyla on the echinoderm-chordate line can show the following characteristics in common with the widely separated annelid-arthropod line:

(*a*) trochophore larva
(*b*) true coelom and chitinous exoskeleton
(*c*) true coelom and endoskeleton
(*d*) true coelom and segmentation.

Q. 117. Which of the following groups does not contain animals which are parasitic in or on man?

(*a*) Protozoa
(*b*) Coelenterata
(*c*) Platyhelminthes
(*d*) Aschelminthes

Q. 118. Members of the phylum Pogonophora

(*a*) are all dioecious
(*b*) are all monoecious
(*c*) are all parthenogenetically reproducing females
(*d*) may be either dioecious or monoecious

Q. 119. In the phylum Pogonophora

(*a*) there is a closed circulatory system
(*b*) there are both fresh-water and marine species

(*c*) there is a mouth but no anus
(*d*) the coelom is a schizocoel.

Q. 120. Connective tissues

(*a*) are made up of densely packed cells
(*b*) are composed of cells embedded in much interceullar material
(*c*) are joined together very tightly
(*d*) consist mainly of spherical cells.

Q. 121. Elastic fibers are present in

(*a*) ligaments
(*b*) tendons
(*c*) bone
(*d*) muscle.

Q. 122. The epidermis of man is an example of a

(*a*) simple columnar epithelium
(*b*) simple cuboidal epithelium
(*c*) stratified cuboidal epithelium
(*d*) stratified squamous epithelium.

Q. 123. The principal tissue of the submucosa of the intestine is

(*a*) muscle
(*b*) columnar ephithelium
(*c*) loose connective tissue
(*d*) ligament.

Q. 124. The wall of the intestine is an example of

(*a*) a tissue
(*b*) an organ
(*c*) an organ system
(*d*) an organism.

Q. 125. Members of the phylum Chaetognatha

(*a*) are all dioecious
(*b*) are all monoecious
(*c*) are all parthenogenetically reproducing females
(*d*) may be either dioecious or monoecious.

Q. 126. In the phylum Chaetognatha

(*a*) three is an open circulatory system
(*b*) there are fresh-water and marine species
(*c*) respiration is by branched gills
(*d*) coelom and mesoderm arise from enterocoelic pouches.

Q. 127. The energy that is actually employed to do work in a process is called

(*a*) endergonic energy
(*b*) exergonic energy
(*c*) free energy
(*d*) stored energy.

Q. 128. Bird and bat wings are

(*a*) both homologous and analogous
(*b*) homologous but not analogous
(*c*) analogous but not homologous.
(*d*) neither homologous nor analogous.

Q. 129. Echinoderms are

(*a*) acoelomate
(*b*) pseudocoelomate
(*c*) schizocoelomate
(*d*) enterocoelomate.

Q. 130. Mollusks are

(*a*) protostomial schizocoelomates
(*b*) deuterostomial schizocoelomates
(*c*) protostomial enterocoelomates
(*d*) deuterostomial enterocoelomates.

Q. 131. Metameric segmentation does not affect the derivatives of

(*a*) ectoderm
(*b*) mesoderm
(*c*) endoderm
(*d*) different germ layers in different animal groups.

Q. 132. The adult mesoderm issues include large amounts of mesenchyme in

(*a*) vertebrates
(*b*) flatworms
(*c*) arthropods
(*d*) lophophorates.

Q. 133. The basic feature of segmentation found in arthropods and annelids as well as the vertebrates

(*a*) shows that annelids are ancestors of vertebrates
(*b*) probably arose independently in the two lines
(*c*) indicates that annelids are specialized types of arthropods
(*d*) shows that the phylogenetic tree must be modified.

Q. 134. Which pair of terms correctly associates the organism and its excretory system (at least in part)?

(*a*) grasshopper–flame cell
(*b*) amoeba–Malpighian tubules
(*c*) grasshopper–excretory contractile vacuole
(*d*) earthworm–chloragen cells.

Q. 135. The following list is arranged in order of increasing phylogenetic complexity.

(*a*) Protozoa, Platyhelminthes, Coelenterata, Aschelminthes, Annelida, Mollusca, Arthropoda
(*b*) Protozoa, Coelenterata, Aschelminthes, Platyhelminthes, Mollusca, Arthropoda, Annelida
(*c*) Protozoa, coelenterata, Platyhelminthes, Mollusca, Aschelminthes, Annelida, Arthropoda
(*d*) Protozoa, Coelenterata, Platyhelminthes, Aschelminthes, Mollusca, Annelida, Arthropoda.

Q. 136. The injection of large quantities of distilled water into a person's veins would cause many of the red blood cells to

(*a*) shrink
(*b*) agglutenate
(*c*) swell and burst
(*d*) carry more oxyen.

Q. 137. Cell organelles that have been identified especially with respiratory activities are

(*a*) nucleoli
(*b*) Golgi bodies
(*c*) chromonemata
(*d*) mitochondria.

Q. 138. In spring and summer, water fleas are

(*a*) self-fertilizing hermaphrodites
(*b*) cross-fertilizing hermaphrodites
(*c*) parthenogenetic
(*d*) separately sexed.

Q. 139. The reduced hind wings of housefiles are

(*a*) elytra
(*b*) cerci
(*c*) halteres
(*d*) trochanters.

Q. 140. Centipedes

(*a*) have poison claws on the first head segment
(*b*) molt throughout life
(*c*) breathe through unbranched tracheal tubes
(*d*) possess two pairs of antennae.

Q. 141. Bettles have mouth parts which are

(*a*) biting and chewing
(*b*) piercing and sucking
(*c*) sucking and lapping
(*d*) functionally different in different groups.

Q. 142. Moths have

(*a*) feathery antennae and horizontally resting wings
(*b*) feathery antennae and vertically upfolded resting wings
(*c*) filamentous antennae and horizontally resting wings
(*d*) filamentous antennae and vertically upfolded resting wings.

Q. 143. Ants are members of the same order as

(*a*) wasps
(*b*) termites

(*c*) butterflies
(*d*) ear wigs.

Q. 144. The transformation from caterpillar to pupa is under the immediate control of the hormones of the

(*a*) corpora allata
(*b*) prothoracic glands
(*c*) cerebral neurosecretory cells
(*d*) sinus glands.

Q. 145. A housefly possesses

(*a*) no skeleton
(*b*) a chitinous exoskeleton
(*c*) a chitinous endoskeleton
(*d*) a horny exoskeleton.

Q. 146. A starfish possesses

(*a*) a chitinous exoskeleton
(*b*) a chitinous endoskeleton
(*c*) a caleareous exoskeleton
(*d*) a calcareous endoskeleton.

Q. 147. Comparatively the largest animals are those with

(*a*) endoskeletons
(*b*) exoskeletons
(*c*) horny skeletons
(*d*) silica skeletons.

Q. 148. A compound eye is

(*a*) found in arthropods and mullusks
(*b*) found in annelids and mollusks
(*c*) found in annelids and arthropods
(*d*) unique to arthropods.

Q. 149. When two hormones function synergistically, they

(*a*) reinforce each other in action
(*b*) oppose each other in action
(*c*) do not influence each other in action
(*d*) inhibit each other in action.

Q. 150. The principal function of the rods of the retina is to

(*a*) enable us to distinguish colors
(*b*) make possible achromatic or colorless vision
(*c*) enable us to see an object from more than one vantage point
(*d*) enable us to get a perception of depth.

Q. 151. The cornea is a continuation of the

(*a*) retina
(*b*) sclera
(*c*) choroid coat
(*d*) iris.

Q. 152. The organ of Corti is located in the

(*a*) utriculus
(*b*) cochlea
(*c*) sacculus
(*d*) middle ear.

Q. 153. In mammals, a substance like adrenalin is secreted by the

(*a*) adrenal cortex
(*b*) nerve endings of the CNS
(*c*) parasympathetic nerve endings
(*d*) sympathetic nerve endings.

Q. 154. Adrenalin in mammals tends to

(*a*) increase heart rate
(*b*) decrease heart rate
(*c*) have no effect on the heart
(*d*) affect only the heart.

Q. 155. Carbohydrate metabolism in vertebrates is regulated

(*a*) in part by insulin
(*b*) solely by insulin
(*c*) in part by pancreatic enzymes
(*d*) solely by pancreatic enzymes.

Q. 156. Spinal nerves of vertebrates contain

(*a*) only sensory fibers

(*b*) only motor fibers
(*c*) sensory and motor fibers
(*d*) only parasympathetic fibers.

Q. 157. In vertebrates, a myelin sheath is absent from

(*a*) sensory nerve fibers
(*b*) motor nerve fibers
(*c*) autonomic nerve fibers
(*d*) nerve fibers of the CNS.

Q. 158. The autonomic nerves which arise from the mid-region of the mammalian spinal cord are

(*a*) sympathetic
(*b*) parasympathetic
(*c*) central
(*d*) cranial.

Q. 159. The iris of vertebrates is a continuation of the

(*a*) retina
(*b*) sclera
(*c*) choroid
(*d*) cornea.

Q. 160. In the axon of a motor fiber the impulse travels

(*a*) toward the eyton
(*b*) away from the cyton
(*c*) toward the dendrites
(*d*) away from a synapse.

Q. 161. In order to carry out a reflex act, a frog must have

(*a*) a spinal cord
(*b*) a spinal cord plus a cerebral cortex
(*c*) a spinal cord plus a medulla oblongata
(*d*) an intact central nervous system.

Q. 162. Insulin promotes the transformation of

(*a*) glucose to glycogen
(*b*) glycogen to glucose
(*c*) a normal person into a diabetic
(*d*) sugar-contraining urine into normal urine.

Q. 163. The anterior lobe of the vertebrate pituitary gland secretes

(*a*) steroid hormones
(*b*) hormones stimulating other endocrine glands
(*c*) hormones which affect smooth muscles
(*d*) hormones which affect skin pigment cells in frogs.

Q. 164. The posterior lobe of the pituitary gland controls

(*a*) nothing in man but pigment cells in frogs
(*b*) the gonads
(*c*) the contraction of some smooth muscles
(*d*) secretion of the thyroid gland.

Q. 165. The hood of an arrowworm

(*a*) aids in scooping food organisms from the water
(*b*) is operated by the smooth muscles of the head region
(*c*) contains a part of the coelom
(*d*) covers the grasping spines when it is retracted.

Q. 166. The coelomic septa of an arrowworm consist of

(*a*) extensions of the epidermal basement membrane
(*b*) periotoneal membranes
(*c*) mesenteric cell sheets
(*d*) connective tissue partitions.

Q. 167. Chaetognaths gastrulate by

(*a*) invagination
(*b*) delamination
(*c*) ingression
(*d*) epiboly.

Q. 168. In arrowworms, the circulatory system is

(*a*) absent
(*b*) open
(*c*) closed
(*d*) patterned differently in different species.

Q. 169. Members of the class Larvaceae

(*a*) are all colonial
(*b*) are solitary, tadpole-like organisms

(*c*) live in a gelatinous secreted housing
(*d*) have no notochord.

Q. 170. Members of the class Ascidiaceae

(*a*) are all solitary
(*b*) have a notochord throughout life
(*c*) are typically dioccious
(*d*) have a tadpole-like larval stage.

Q. 171. Cephalochordates

(*a*) have a notochord only in the larval stage
(*b*) have no head or brain
(*c*) are unsegmented
(*d*) are sessile as adults.

Q. 172. The authors of the cell theory were

(*a*) Hooke and Brown
(*b*) Schleiden and Schwann
(*c*) Dujardin and von Mohl
(*d*) Schleiden and Schultze.

Q. 173. When an amoeba has been cut into two parts, the part without the nucleus

(*a*) a reproduces
(*b*) dies immediately
(*c*) regenerates a new amoeba
(*d*) lives for some time but cannot reproduce.

Q. 174. The longest human nerve cell with its processes may measure about

(*a*) 1*u*
(*b*) 7.5*u*
(*c*) 3 in.
(*d*) 3-4 feet.

Q. 175. The structure of the eye which is altered in the defect known as astigmatism is

(*a*) cornea
(*b*) lens
(*c*) iris
(*d*) A and B above.

Q. 176. Dim stars are seen when you are not directly focusing on them because

(*a*) the lens flattens for far-vision
(*b*) cones are abundant near the periphery of the retina
(*c*) rods are abundant near the periphery of the retina
(*d*) cones are more light-sensitive than rods.

Q. 177. The sense associated with tension in muscles and tendons is

(*a*) resonation
(*b*) proprioception
(*c*) tentaculation
(*d*) correlation.

Q. 178. Endocrine glands secrete

(*a*) into ducts
(*b*) into the body fluids
(*c*) into the intestine
(*d*) through the pituitary.

Q. 179. Gonadotropic hormones

(*a*) are secreted by the gonads
(*b*) stimulate the pituitary to produce gonadal hormones
(*c*) inhibit the gonads from producing estrogen
(*d*) are secreted by the pituitary.

Q. 180. The cerebellum is the seat of

(*a*) intelligence
(*b*) sensory perception
(*c*) motor coordination
(*d*) pathway facilitation.

Q. 181. A nervous impulse

(*a*) is an electric current
(*b*) is an energy-consuming process
(*c*) travels with the speed of electricity
(*d*) is due to diffusion of acetyleholine or adrenalin.

Q. 182. The hormone of the parathyroid gland regulates

(a) thyroid secretions
(b) calcium metabolism
(c) the growth rate of a vertebrate
(d) respiration rate.

Q. 183. Dermal scales are encountered in

(a) fishes
(b) reptiles
(c) birds
(d) mammals.

Q. 184. Bone substance may be resorbed by

(a) chondroblasts
(b) periostea
(c) osteoclasts
(d) perichondria.

Q. 185. The eye of a squid is an example of a

(a) spot ocellus
(b) cup ocellus
(c) vesicular ocellus
(d) ommatidium.

Q. 186. Some workers place the bacteria and the blue-green algae in the kingdom Monera because they lack

(a) plasma membranes
(b) ribosomes
(c) chromatin material
(d) nuclear envelopes.

Q. 187. Given here are numbered taxonomic categories 1. kingdom; 2. order; 3. species; 4. family; 5. class; 6. genus; 7. phylum. Which of the following series gives the categories in proper sequence (highest to lowest)?

(a) 1 2 7 5 4 6 3
(b) 1 7 5 2 4 6 3
(c) 1 2 5 6 4 7 3
(d) 1 7 2 5 4 6 3.

Q. 188. Which of the following includes all of the others?

(*a*) class
(*b*) genus
(*c*) order
(*d*) species.

Q. 189. The four recognized stages of complete metamorphosis are (in order)

(*a*) egg, nymph, pupa, adult
(*b*) egg, larva, naiad, adult
(*c*) egg, naiad, larva, adult
(*d*) egg, larva, pupa, adult.

Q. 190. A spider differs from an insect in that the spider

(*a*) lacks locomotor appendages on the abdomen
(*b*) has eight legs
(*c*) has a hard external skeleton
(*d*) reproduces by internal fertilization.

Q. 191. The centipedes and millipedes differ from the insects in which one of the following respects?

(*a*) their head segments are fused
(*b*) they have jointed legs
(*c*) they have segmented antennae
(*d*) they have more than six legs.

Q. 192. *Acetabularia* is a

(*a*) unicellular plant
(*b*) unicellular animal
(*c*) multicellular plant
(*d*) multicellular animal.

Q. 193. Bone in a live animal

(*a*) is nonliving
(*b*) contains active cells
(*c*) is a form of epithelial tissue
(*d*) is not a tissue.

Q. 194. The cell principle as now used states that

(*a*) cells have nuclei
(*b*) cells, with a few exceptions, are composed of cells and/or nuclei

(*c*) organisms are composed of one or more cells and cell products
(*d*) plants are composed of cells.

Q. 195. Barnacles·

(*a*) become attached on their larval first antennae
(*b*) have phyllopodial legs
(*c*) develop via nauplius larvae
(*d*) possess well developed abdominal legs

Q. 196. The principal swimming organs in water fleas are

(*a*) maxillae
(*b*) antennae
(*c*) thoracic legs
(*d*) abdomen and telson.

Q. 197. Malacostraca are characterized uniquely by the presence of

(*a*) abdominal appendages
(*b*) six segments in the thorax
(*c*) a head and thorax-covering carapace
(*d*) gonopores on the first abdominal segment.

Q. 198. The swimmerets of a lobster

(*a*) serve as copulatory organs in males
(*b*) carry developing eggs in females
(*c*) propel the animal backward
(*d*) are uniramous abdominal appendages.

Q. 199. Adrenalin causes the mammalian heart to

(*a*) slow down
(*b*) accelerate
(*c*) stop altogether
(*d*) pump erratically.

Q. 200. Blood platelets in mammals

(*a*) grow into red blood corpuscles
(*b*) grow into white blood cells
(*c*) initiate blood clooting
(*d*) release fibrinogen in blood clotting.

Section III

Q. 201. The longest intestines, comparatively, are found in

(*a*) carnivores
(*b*) herbivores
(*c*) omnivores
(*d*) elongated worm-shaped animals.

Q. 202. In mammals, blood from the lungs flows

(*a*) into the left ventricle
(*b*) into the right ventricle
(*c*) through the pulmonary artery
(*d*) through the pulmonary vein.

Q. 203. Clotting of human blood

(*a*) requires that pepsinogen be present
(*b*) results from fibrin joining with globulin
(*c*) is the result of platelets releasing fibrinogen
(*d*) depends on the formation of the thrombin from prothrombin.

Q. 204. Vertebrate lymphocytes

(*a*) engulf bacteria
(*b*) are antibodies
(*c*) are of doubtful function
(*d*) are formed in bone marrow.

Q. 205. The inner lining of all blood vessels in a closed circulation is

(*a*) the mesothelium
(*b*) the pericardium
(*c*) the endothelium
(*d*) a capillary.

Q. 206. The blood pigment of most crustacea is

(*a*) hemoglobin
(*b*) hemerythrin
(*c*) hemocyanin
(*d*) chlorocruorin.

Q. 207. One blood component normally unable to pass into capsular urine during nephric filtration in vertebrates is

(*a*) blood glucose
(*b*) blood protein
(*c*) salt
(*d*) urea.

Q. 208. Among blood pigments, the most efficient oxygen-carrier is

(*a*) hemoglobin
(*b*) hemerythrin
(*c*) hemocyanin
(*d*) chlorocruorin.

Q. 209. Breathing by tracheal tubes occurs in

(*a*) most invertebrates
(*b*) earth worms
(*c*) insects
(*d*) flatworms.

Q. 210. Crossopteryian or lobe-finned fish are noteworthy because

(*a*) they died out with no descendants
(*b*) they are rare examples of parasitic fish
(*c*) the amphibia arose from this group
(*d*) they live in cocoons during the dry season.

Q. 211. Scales which are modifications of the integument and differ from fish scales

(*a*) are found in reptiles only
(*b*) are first found in amphibia
(*c*) are found in reptiles, birds and mammals
(*d*) are found in reptiles and birds.

Q. 212. In order to identify and distinguish a fossil mammal from a fossil reptile a modestly informed biologist would

(*a*) know for sure if he recognized that only one bone composed the lower jaw
(*b*) have to see the skull
(*c*) would need to find remnants of the integument
(*d*) would have to run tests which would tell what the usual environmental temperature had been.

Q. 213. A hypotonic urine is formed by

(*a*) mammals
(*b*) birds
(*c*) freshwater fishes
(*d*) insects.

Q. 214. Proteins normally present in a blood

(*a*) represent foods in transit to cells
(*b*) are formed from proteins absorbed from the gut
(*c*) have no known function
(*d*) are formed from amino acids absorbed from the gut.

Q. 215. In a mammal, puncture of the thoracic wall, but not of the lung itself, will cause

(*a*) collapse of the lung
(*b*) inflation of the lung
(*c*) no substantial interference with breathing
(*d*) increased rates of breathing.

Q. 216. Carbon monoxide is toxic to vertebrates because it

(*a*) saturates the plasma
(*b*) forms a stable compound with hemoglobin
(*c*) prevents passage of red corpuscles through the capillaries
(*d*) cannot diffuse out of the lungs.

Q. 217. In man, the lungs are caused to inflate by

(*a*) contraction of muscles in their walls
(*b*) contraction of the diaphragm
(*c*) relaxation of the chest muscles
(*d*) relaxation of chest and abdomen.

Q. 218. Venous blood becomes arterial

(*a*) in the lungs
(*b*) in the tissues
(*c*) when HbO_2 releases oxygen
(*d*) when HCO_3^- is formed.

Q. 219. The immediate cause of inhalation in man is

(*a*) increase in blood CO_2

(*b*) a series of nerve impulses from the breathing center
(*c*) exhalation
(*d*) contraction of breathing muscles.

Q. 220. The immediate cause of exhalation in man is
(*a*) inhibition of the breathing center
(*b*) nerve impulses from the lungs to the breathing center
(*c*) recoil of the lung alveoli
(*d*) nerve impulses from the breathing center to the diaphragm.

Q. 221. In vertebrates, liver cells
(*a*) are the only ones capable of manufacturing essential amino acids
(*b*) are the only ones capable of manufacuting essential fatty acids
(*c*) are specialized for water storage
(*d*) are specialized for the storage of certain vitamins.

Q. 222. Fats absorbed into the vertebrate lymph circulation
(*a*) end up in adipose tissues
(*b*) end up in the liver
(*c*) are utilized immediately as fuel
(*d*) end up in the lacteals.

Q. 223. The metacoels of beardworms communicate with the exterior
(*a*) by no openings
(*b*) by nephridiopores
(*c*) by gonopores
(*d*) indirectly via the mesocoels.

Q. 224. The mesocoels of acorn worms communicate with the exterior via
(*a*) no openings
(*b*) proboscis pores
(*c*) neuropores
(*d*) gill pores.

Q. 225. The main nervous system of starfishes is the
(*a*) ectoneural system

(*b*) endoneural system
(*c*) hyponeural system
(*d*) epineural system.

Q. 226. The echinoderm organ most nearly equivalent to a heart is the

(*a*) axial sinus
(*b*) madreporic ampulla
(*c*) axial gland
(*d*) ring sinus.

Q. 227. A sea cucumber typically develops via a larval type known as a

(*a*) aurecularia
(*b*) brachiolaria
(*c*) bipinnaria
(*d*) doliolaria.

Q. 228. Brittle stars differ from other echinoderms in the

(*a*) presence of epineural canals
(*b*) absence of intestines
(*c*) presence of viviparous species
(*d*) absence of madreporites.

Q. 229. Asteroids are characterized by

(*a*) bursal slits
(*b*) Cuverian tubules
(*c*) Aristotle's lanterns
(*d*) pyloric caeca.

Q. 230. Asteroids excrete by means of

(*a*) glomeruli
(*b*) madreporites
(*c*) coelomic amoebocytes
(*d*) metanephridial tubules.

Q. 231. The endoneural nervous system of a starfish lies closest to the

(*a*) genital ring sinus
(*b*) radial sinus

(*c*) hyponeural ring sinus
(*d*) axial sinus.

Q. 232. An echinoderm structure not forming part of the water-vascular system is a

(*a*) madreporic vesicle
(*b*) podial ampulla
(*c*) madreporic ampulla
(*d*) podium.

Q. 233. The phylum with presumably the greatest evolutionary affinity to the hypothetical dipleurula like ancestors of deuterostomes is that of the

(*a*) Branchiata
(*b*) Chordata
(*c*) Echinodermata
(*d*) Hemichordata.

Q. 234. The echinoderm water-vascular system probably has evolutionary affinity to the pterobranch

(*a*) protosome
(*b*) branching black stolon
(*c*) ciliary bands of the larval
(*d*) mesosomal tentacles.

Q. 235. The compound eye

(*a*) is of little value to the organism
(*b*) is a degenerate form of the camera eye
(*c*) is characteristic of annelids and mollusks
(*d*) produces a mosaic image.

Q. 236. The crustacean head is composed of how many segments?

(*a*) 2
(*b*) 3
(*c*) 4
(*d*) 5

Q. 237. If you were looking at some cells under a microscope, they could be identified as animal cells if they contained

(*a*) nuclei

(*b*) chromosomes
(*c*) vacuoles
(*d*) no cell walls.

Q. 238. The principle layer of the intestine in which one finds blood vessels, lymph vessels, and lymph glands is the

(*a*) mucosa
(*b*) submucosa
(*c*) circular muscle layer
(*d*) longitudinal muscle layer.

Q. 239. A human cell type that is an example of a syncytium is

(*a*) nerve
(*b*) smooth muscle
(*c*) striated muscle
(*d*) columnar epithelium.

Q. 240. The plasma membrane of a living cell is

(*a*) the very thin outermost region of the cytoplasm
(*b*) the innermost layer of the cell wall
(*c*) a layer bounding the vacuole
(*d*) a layer in which all metabolism is carried on.

Q. 241. The endoderm of an embryo gives rise to

(*a*) the nervous system
(*b*) the lining of the digestive system
(*c*) muscles, blood, and bone
(*d*) the reproductive system.

Q. 242. The ectoderm of an embryo gives rise to

(*a*) the nervous system
(*b*) the lining of the digestive system
(*c*) the muscular system
(*d*) the reproductive system.

Q. 243. When the eye-cup of a salamander embryo is cut out early in development, it will

(*a*) induce the formation of a whole eye
(*b*) prevent all eyes from forming
(*c*) degenerate completely
(*d*) induce the formation of a lens.

Q. 244. Natural parthenogenesis

(*a*) is unknown
(*b*) occurs when a frog egg is pricked with a needle
(*c*) is common among rotifers and other animals
(*d*) means normal development of fertilized eggs.

Q. 245. The chief factor in the production of black or humus soils is the action of

(*a*) running water
(*b*) differential erosion
(*c*) bacteria on organic material
(*d*) cultivation and grazing.

Q. 246. Which of the following species of animals is likely to be found over a wider range of climatic conditions than any of the others?

(*a*) fox
(*b*) snake
(*c*) salamander
(*d*) frog.

Q. 247. An environment which could not be inhabited by any kind of organism is one which lacks

(*a*) access to free nitrogen molecules
(*b*) access to carbon in any form
(*c*) access to free oxygen molecules
(*d*) access to light.

Q. 248. Certain species of desert lizards excrete their wastes in dry form. The represents

(*a*) a limiting factor of the organism
(*b*) adaptation of the organism to environment
(*c*) a protective device against enemies
(*d*) the result of malnutrition.

Q. 249. The microscopic organisms living near the surface of water, either fresh or salt, are known collectively as

(*a*) microbes
(*b*) kelps

(*c*) plankton
(*d*) blue-green algae.

Q. 250. The excretory organs of *Peripatus*

(*a*) resemble annelid nephridia
(*b*) resemble Malpighian tubules
(*c*) resemble cephalopod kidneys
(*d*) resemble chordate solenocytes.

Q. 251. The following characteristics of *Peripatus*, taken together, clearly indicate the relationship between this animal and the phylum Arthropoda:

(*a*) segmented appendages, trachea present, open circulatory system, claws present
(*b*) claws present, trachea present, open circulatory system
(*c*) closed circulatory system, nephridia present, trachea present, claws present
(*d*) claws present, trachea present, nephridia present, open circulatory system.

Q. 252. The neurilemma is

(*a*) fatty covering around nerve fibers
(*b*) a cellular covering around nerve fibers
(*c*) an individual axon fiber
(*d*) a myelin envelope.

Q. 253. Spinal nerves contain

(*a*) only sensory fibers
(*b*) only motor fibers
(*c*) sensory and motor fibers
(*d*) only parasympathetic fibers.

Q. 254. Neurons can be classified into the following groups:

(*a*) sensory, afferent, association
(*b*) sensory, association, motor
(*c*) efferent, association, motor
(*d*) sensory, afferent, motor.

Q. 255. In vertibrates, the first organ system laid down in embryonic form is the

(*a*) nervous system
(*b*) skeletal system
(*c*) alimentary system
(*d*) integumentary system.

Q. 256. The development of transparency in embryonic lens tissue is an instance of

(*a*) morphogenesis
(*b*) form regulating movements
(*c*) differentiation
(*d*) growth.

Q. 257. The event terminating the embryonic phase in most animals is

(*a*) gastrulation
(*b*) hatching
(*c*) metamorphosis
(*d*) birth.

Q. 258. One process which occurs in common in both sexual and asexual patterns of development is

(*a*) formation of a larva
(*b*) morphogenesis
(*c*) fertilization
(*d*) gastrulation.

Q. 259. The first demonstrable event in the development of a fertilized animal egg is

(*a*) induction
(*b*) establishment of polarity
(*c*) cleavage
(*d*) establishment of spherical symmetry.

Q. 260. Mammalian eggs are

(*a*) isolecithal
(*b*) centrolecithal
(*c*) telolecithal
(*d*) discoidal.

Q. 261. Coeloblastulae with large blastocoels generally gastrulate by

(*a*) ingression
(*b*) delamination
(*c*) invagination
(*d*) epiboly.

Q. 262. An animal is classified as protostomial or deuterostomial according to the fate of the

(*a*) archenteron
(*b*) blastocoel
(*c*) mesoderm
(*d*) blastopore.

Q. 263. In hemichordates, a notochord

(*a*) is absent
(*b*) develops in larval stages only
(*c*) is represented by the stomocord
(*d*) persists in the form of the adult collar cord.

Q. 264. Among living echinoderms, the mouth lies on the oral side in

(*a*) crinoids only
(*b*) groups with open ambulacral grooves only
(*c*) all groups except the sea cucumbers
(*d*) all groups.

Q. 265. The structure of *Peripatus* suggests strongly that

(*a*) ancestral annelids are closely related
(*b*) mollusks and annelids are closely related
(*c*) arthropods were primitively aquatic
(*d*) arthropods and annelids had a common ancestor.

Q. 266. Members of the phylum Tardigrada

(*a*) have segmented appendages
(*b*) have a well-developed tracheal respiratory system
(*c*) lack a chitinous cuticle
(*d*) are parasites of nasal passages of carnivorous vertebrates as adults.

Q. 267. Members of the phylum Pentastomida

(*a*) have 4 pairs of segmented appendages

(*b*) are parasites of nasal passages of carnivorous vertebrates as adults
(*c*) lack a chitinous cuticle
(*d*) have an open circulatory system.

Q. 268. The first heart part to receive the blood in embryos and in the adults of some more ancient vertebrates is

(*a*) atrium
(*b*) sinus venosus
(*c*) ventricle
(*d*) conus arteriosus.

Q. 269. In the frog's heart, blood

(*a*) passes from auricle to right ventricle
(*b*) passes from sinus venosus to conus arteriosus
(*c*) passes from both atria into a common ventricle
(*d*) must pass to the lungs.

Q. 270. The red blood corpuscle count in normal humans ranges between

(*a*) 2×10^6 and 4×10^6
(*b*) 4×10^6 and 6×10^6
(*c*) 6×10^6 and 8×10^6
(*d*) 8×10^6 and 10×10^6.

Q. 271. Blood proteins are present in the blood in the following relative concentrations

(*a*) serum albumin > serum globulin > fibrinogen
(*b*) serum albumin < serum globulin < fibrinogen
(*c*) fibrinogen > serum albumin > serum globulin
(*d*) serum globulin < fibrinogen < serum albumin.

Q. 272. Chromosomes are

(*a*) not visible during the resting stage
(*b*) not present during the resting stage
(*c*) present only during the resting stage
(*d*) broken up during the resting stage.

Q. 273. UDP appears to be a specific raw material in the manufacture of

(*a*) DNA
(*b*) RNA
(*c*) both DNA and RNA
(*d*) neither DNA nor RNA.

Q. 274. Activation of amino acids requires the direct participation of

(*a*) messenger RNA
(*b*) chromosomal RNA
(*c*) ribosomal RNA
(*d*) transfer RNA.

Q. 275. A uracil triplet appears to constitute the specific genetic code for

(*a*) histidine
(*b*) leucine
(*c*) valine
(*d*) phenyl alamine.

Q. 276. According to the operon hypothesis, code transcription to *m*RNA is achieved by

(*a*) operator genes
(*b*) structural genes
(*c*) regulator genes
(*d*) recessive genes.

Q. 277. Which of the following gives evidence that animals living in groups, even though unorganized, have a better chance of survival than those living alone?

(*a*) When geese migrate the flock follows the leader
(*b*) When a herd of deer is grazing the individuals alternate in maintaining a lockout for enemies
(*c*) In a bee-hive the queen takes over reproductive duties in which the drone assists, while sterile females are the workers charged with the responsibility
(*d*) A large group of fish can tolerate an amount of poison in the water that would kill a very few.

Q. 278. The most important producers throughout the ocean are

(*a*) red and brown algae

(*b*) diatoms
(*c*) red algae and photosynthetic flagellates
(*d*) diatoms and photosynthetic flagellates.

Q. 279. The typhlosole is important to the earthworm because

(*a*) it reinforces the dorsal side of the organism
(*b*) it contains the main nerve trunks
(*c*) it increases the absorptive area of the gut
(*d*) it houses the main sex organs.

Q. 280. Phylum Annelida includes

(*a*) flatworms, roundworms and rotifers
(*b*) sandworms, earthworms and rotifers
(*c*) sandworms, earthworms and roundworms
(*d*) sandworms, earthworms and leeches.

Q. 281. The annelids possess

(*a*) a tube-within-a-tube body plan, a true coelom and a closed circulatory system
(*b*) a tube-within-a-tube body plan, a true coelom and an open circulatory system
(*c*) a true coelom, a pseudocoel and an open circulatory system
(*d*) a pseudocoel, an open circulatory system and a ladder type nervous system.

Q. 282. Class Polychaeta includes the common sandworm and it is characterized by

(*a*) many jaws
(*b*) few bristles (satae)
(*c*) many bristles (setae)
(*d*) lack of setae.

Q. 283. In addition to nephridia, which of the following also has excretory function in the earthworm?

(*a*) typhlosole
(*b*) chloragen cells
(*c*) calciferous glands
(*d*) gizzard.

Q. 284. Frog's blood differs from man's in its *route of return* from the leg

(*a*) in being able to pass blood along by two major routes
(*b*) in being obligated to pass through the kidneys
(*c*) in being forced through a portal system by one route of travel, not the other
(*d*) in having accessory "hearts" in the things to push the blood along.

Q. 285. Immunity is

(*a*) a development of recent science
(*b*) a line of defense
(*c*) always the result of thromboplastin
(*d*) the application of law to biology.

Q. 286. The heart in humans

(*a*) lacks semilunar valves
(*b*) lacks autonomic nervous system
(*c*) always lacked a sinus venosus
(*d*) delivers blood to two major areas simultaneously, on contraction.

Q. 287. Metameric segmentation is characteristic of

(*a*) all craniate chordates
(*b*) all acraniate chordates
(*c*) tadpoles but not adults of ascidians
(*d*) tadpoles of all indirectly developing tunicates.

Q. 288. From the pharynx, water in an ascidian passes directly into the

(*a*) atrial siphon
(*b*) branchial basket
(*c*) peribranchial cavity
(*d*) branchial siphon.

Q. 289. The apicardium of an ascidian is not known to

(*a*) arise from endoderm
(*b*) form the heart
(*c*) contribute to bud formation
(*d*) give rise to excretory structures.

Q. 290. If a crustacean hatches at an extremely late developmental stage, it will emerge as a

(*a*) nauplius
(*b*) pluteus
(*c*) zoaea
(*d*) adult.

Q. 291. Frog eggs are

(*a*) isolecithal
(*b*) centrolecithal
(*c*) telolecithal
(*d*) discoidal.

Q. 292. Mollusk eggs cleave

(*a*) radially
(*b*) bilaterally
(*c*) spirally
(*d*) irregularly.

Q. 293. Vertebrate eggs cleave

(*a*) radially
(*b*) bilaterally
(*c*) spirally
(*d*) irregularly

Q. 294. A chorion is not encountered in

(*a*) frogs
(*b*) reptiles
(*c*) birds
(*d*) mammals.

Q. 295. Muscle contraction, according to the currently most widely accepted theory

(*a*) involves the movement of *actin fibers* in toward the center of the *sarcomere*
(*b*) involves the movement of myosin fibers in toward the center of the sarcomere
(*c*) occurs by the compressive action of the Z-lines
(*d*) results from folding in the H-zone.

Q. 296. A single muscle twitch

(*a*) is the product of contraction immediately upon stimulation
(*b*) is a contraction following a relaxation period during which the fibers collect oxygen
(*c*) is preceded by a latent period after stimulation
(*d*) is inhibited by the presence of oxygen.

Q. 297. From shoulder to fingertips the sequence of bones is

(*a*) phalanges, carpels, metacarpels, radius-ulna, humerus
(*b*) phalanges, metacarpets, radius-ulna, humerus
(*c*) radius-ulna, humerus, carpels, metacarpels, phalanges
(*d*) humerus, radius-ulna, carpels, metacarpels, phalanges.

Q. 298. The human egg falls into the classification of

(*a*) small and equally distributed yolk
(*b*) moderate amount of yolk in higher concentration at the vegetal pole
(*c*) highly yolkladen with a cap of active cytoplasm at the animal pole.
(*d*) having its yolk centrally enclosed in cytoplasmic rind.

Q. 299. Gene mutations in the sex chromosomes of man would tend to become visibly expressed

(*a*) more frequently in males
(*b*) more frequently in females
(*c*) equally frequently in both sexes
(*d*) as frequently as autosomal mutations.

Q. 300. In mammals, a pair of sex chromosomes is present in

(*a*) germs cells only
(*b*) somatic cells only
(*c*) every cell in the body except mature gametes
(*d*) every cell.

Section IV

Q. 301. Mendel's law of segregation implies that the two members of an allelic pair of genes

(*a*) are distributed to separate gametes
(*b*) may contaminate one another
(*c*) are assorted independently of all other genes
(*d*) are segregated pairwise.

Q. 302. If a normal body cell of the fruit fly *Drosophila* has eight chromosomes

(*a*) each sperm has eight
(*b*) the haploid number is eight
(*c*) each egg has four
(*d*) eight chromosomes go into each polar body.

Q. 303. If a character is sex-linked, it follows that the gene or genes determining it are located on

(*a*) the Y chromosome
(*b*) the X chromosome
(*c*) on both sex chromosomes
(*d*) on autosomes only.

Q. 304. The behaviour of chromosomes during meiosis and the behaviour of genes are

(*a*) in general, somewhat alike
(*b*) identical
(*c*) different, at least in some respects
(*d*) not related.

Q. 305. Irradiation of cells with X rays

(*a*) always kills them
(*b*) has no effect at low doses
(*c*) will increase the mutation rate
(*d*) always causes lethal mutations.

Q. 306. If Mr. and Mrs. Smith have two boys and one girl, the chances that the next child to be born will be a girl are

(*a*) 1/3

(*b*) 1/4
(*c*) 2/3
(*d*) 1/2.

Q. 307. Genes are thought to be located in the chromosomes

(*a*) because hereditary traits are distributed like chromosomes during meiosis
(*b*) because with special techniques genes can be seen in the chromosomes
(*c*) because of Mendel's predictions inherent in his laws
(*d*) because genes consist of nucleoproteins.

Q. 308. The normal cell of a diploid animal usually contains

(*a*) a Y chromosome
(*b*) a single X chromosome
(*c*) two of most kinds of chromosomes
(*d*) one of most kinds of chromosomes.

Q. 309. If two animals heterozygous for a given character are mated, the resulting offspring will be expected to exhibit a genotype ratio of

(*a*) 3:1
(*b*) 1:2:2:1
(*c*) 1:2:1
(*d*) 9:3:3:1.

Q. 310. Sex is determined in man

(*a*) by the ratio of X chromosomes to other chromosomes
(*b*) by sex linkage
(*c*) by the absence of a Y chromosome
(*d*) by the presence of a Y chromosome.

Q. 311. Mutations occur

(*a*) in every cell
(*b*) whenever genes are hit by highenergy radiation
(*c*) at the same rate in all genes
(*d*) in unpredictable fashion.

Q. 312. Mendel arrived at a clear understanding of heredity before a satisfactory theory was available because

(*a*) he studied one trait at a time
(*b*) he had unlimited funds
(*c*) he was aware of the behaviour of chromosomes
(*d*) he was unaware of the behaviour of chromosomes.

Q. 313. Certain termites eat wood but are unable to digest the wood without the aid of flagellate protozoans which live in their intestines. The protozoans are in turn unable to live outside the bodies of termites. This is an example of

(*a*) commensalism
(*b*) symbiosis
(*c*) saprophytism
(*d*) parasitism.

Q. 314. Animals at the top of a food chain

(*a*) breed faster than those lower in the food chain
(*b*) are smaller than those lower in the food chain
(*c*) are generally more numerous than those lower in the chain
(*d*) are carnivores.

Q. 315. Three important characteristics of annelids are

(*a*) segmentation, coelom, trochophore larvae
(*b*) segmentation, pseudocoel, trochophore larvae
(*c*) segmentation, coelom, longitudinal muscles only
(*d*) segmentation, dorsal hollow nervous system, coelom.

Q. 316. Copulation in the earthworm involves

(*a*) mutual exchange of sperm
(*b*) mutual exchange of eggs
(*c*) mutual exchange of sperm and eggs
(*d*) unidirectional transfer of sperm.

Q. 317. The earthworm differs from *Neanthes (Nereis)* in that it lacks

(*a*) chitinous structures
(*b*) separation of the sexes
(*c*) well-developed head
(*d*) closed circulatory system.

Q. 318. The structure in annelids which provides increased absorptive surface in the digestive system is

(*a*) clitellum
(*b*) septum
(*c*) typhlosole
(*d*) coelom.

Q. 319. The phenotype of an animal can be determined

(*a*) by test-breeding
(*b*) by testing for linkage
(*c*) if it is a homozygous recessive
(*d*) by looking at it.

Q. 320. The discovery that mutations could be induced artificially depended upon

(*a*) the discovery of X rays
(*b*) finding a technique for counting legal mutations
(*c*) finding a technique for counting visible mutations
(*d*) unlimited funds.

Q. 321. Lethal mutations are those mutations which

(*a*) can never be inherited
(*b*) have no visible effect on the organism
(*c*) cause death during embryonic development
(*d*) occur rarely.

Q. 322. Hemophilia in man is rarely seen in females because

(*a*) it is sex-linked and normally expresses itself only in males
(*b*) it is usually lethal when the female becomes sexually mature
(*c*) females do not carry the gene in question
(*d*) the gene in question is located on the Y chromosome.

Q. 323. In man, the character "color-blindness" is a

(*a*) sex-linked recessive
(*b*) Mendelian dominant
(*c*) sex-linked dominant
(*d*) genotype.

Q. 324. The mutation rate of an organism may be increased by

(*a*) no known means
(*b*) almost any kind of external treatment
(*c*) most things which affect the mother
(*d*) treatment with X rays.

Q. 325. Mendel's law of independent assortment states that

(a) there is a blending of heredity in each generation
(*b*) allelic traits tend to mix
(*c*) non-allelic traits are inherited independently
(*d*) chromosomes are the carriers of hereditary material.

Q. 326. Mutations are

(*a*) stable changes in the genetic substance
(*b*) non-hereditary environmental variations
(*c*) rarely harmful
(*d*) usually drastic reorganizations of animal structure and/or function.

Q. 327. It is probaole that in a cell

(*a*) genes do not influence one another
(*b*) all genes influence one another
(*c*) only genes in one chromosome influence one another
(*d*) paternal genes influence only maternal genes, and vice versa.

Q. 328. The antigen, Rh, is found in Rhesus monkeys and

(*a*) in all humans
(*b*) in more than 3/4 of all humans
(*c*) in about half of all humans
(*d*) in about one fourth of all humans.

Q. 329. Animals that receive grafts before or just after birth and retain them for the remainder of their lives

(*a*) are called hypersensitive
(*b*) possess auto-immunity
(*c*) possess anaphylaxis
(*d*) are called tolerant.

Q. 330. Neutrophils are

(*a*) red cells neutralized and stationary along capillary walls
(*b*) known to defibrinate blood
(*c*) the same size as platelets
(*d*) a class of leucocytes.

Q. 331. The engulfing of liquids at the surface of a cell is called

(*a*) phagocytosis
(*b*) blastocytosis
(*c*) pinocytosis
(*d*) monocytosis.

Q. 332. Modifications of adjacent plasma membranes that bind them together are

(*a*) desmosomes
(*b*) quantasomes
(*c*) lysosomes
(*d*) dictyosomes.

Q. 333. The blood of amphioxus contains

(*a*) neither cells nor pigments
(*b*) hemoglobin within cells
(*c*) red cells and white cells
(*d*) pigments dissolved in plasma.

Q. 334. Excretory structures such as are present in amphioxus are

(*a*) found nowhere else
(*b*) segmental nephridia
(*c*) homologous to the primitive vertebrate pronephros
(*d*) flame bulb systems.

Q. 335. Amphioxus development includes

(*a*) mosaic eggs
(*b*) coeloblastulae
(*c*) epibolic gastrulation
(*d*) segmental endomesodermal somites without coelomic cavities.

Q. 336. In amphioxus, the notochord arises

(*a*) by invagination of a longitudinal fold from the dorsal ectoderm
(*b*) by anterior proliferation of a strand of dorsal mesoderm cells from the blastopore region
(*c*) from the middorsal portion of the archenteron
(*d*) between the segmental splanchnocoels on each side of the body.

Q. 337. In early amphioxus larvae

(*a*) the mouth is on the right and the gill slits are on the left
(*b*) an atrium is not present
(*c*) the first gill slits formed are originally unpaired
(*d*) gills slits are not present.

Q. 338. In a larvacean, water flow through the animal is maintained by the

(*a*) cilia in the pharyngeal lining
(*b*) endostyle
(*c*) grid-and-flap system in the windows of the housing
(*d*) movements of the tail.

Q. 339. Vertebrates appear to have evolved from ancestral

(*a*) cephalochordates
(*b*) ascidians
(*c*) larvaceans
(*d*) thaliaceans.

Q. 340. Individuals carrying two of the same alleles are said to be

(*a*) hybrids
(*b*) dominant
(*c*) haploid
(*d*) homozygous.

Q. 341. If nonallelic genes are on different chromosomes, they are

(*a*) inherited independently
(*b*) linked
(*c*) always segregated
(*d*) arranged in linear order.

Q. 342. Recessive genes located in the X chromosome are always

(*a*) dominant
(*b*) expressed in males
(*c*) recessive lethals
(*d*) expressed in females.

Q. 343. A man could inherit from

(*a*) 23
(*b*) 46
(*c*) 92
(*d*) an enormous number, of his ancestors.

Q. 344. If a normal woman produces sons with hemophilia (caused by the sex-linked recessive gene *h*), her genotype must be

(*a*) HH
(*b*) Hh
(*c*) hh
(*d*) undeterminable.

Q. 345. The smallest genetic unit capable of undergoing a stable change is a

(*a*) gene
(*b*) cistron
(*c*) muton
(*d*) recon.

Q. 346. In mammals, a sex-linked trait is one which is usually produced by a gene in

(*a*) the Y chromosome
(*b*) any autosome
(*c*) the X chromosome
(*d*) chromosomes which cross over.

Q. 347. Alleles are genes which

(*a*) are linked
(*b*) are lethal when homozygous
(*c*) occupy corresponding places in corresponding chromosomes
(*d*) are never heterozygous.

Q. 348. If the factor *A* is essential for sight and the factor *B* results in blindness no matter what other genes are present, then the ratio of blind to normal offspring of the cross *aaBb* X *Aabb* will be

(*a*) 1:1
(*b*) 2:1
(*c*) 3:1
(*d*) 1:3.

Q. 349. A color-blind woman is

(*a*) an impossibility
(*b*) less likely than a color-blind man
(*c*) difficult to account for
(*d*) the only type of color-blind condition possible.

Q. 350. The linear arrangement of genes makes possible

(*a*) the occurrence of independent assortment
(*b*) the close approximation of allelic genes during meiosis
(*c*) the phenomena of dominance and recessiveness
(*d*) the occurrence of segregation.

Q. 351. A genotype consisting of two identical genes for a given character is said to be

(*a*) dominant
(*b*) homozygous
(*c*) recessive
(*d*) heterozygous.

Q. 352. In man, a fertilized egg is destined to become a female if

(*a*) it is fertilized within the body cavity of the female
(*b*) an X-bearing egg is fertilized by an X-bearing sperm
(*c*) an X-bearing egg is fertilized by a Y-bearing sperm
(*d*) an XX-bearing egg is fertilized by an XY-bearing sperm.

Q. 353. In n=3 in a given animal, the number of genetically different types of gametes the animal can produce is

(*a*) 2
(*b*) 4

(*c*) 6
(*d*) 8.

Q. 354. Gene mutations are

(*a*) mostly dominant
(*b*) mostly beneficial
(*c*) mostly due to X rays
(*d*) mostly recessive.

Q. 355. The temperature range for the life processes in most organisms is between

(*a*) 10°-50°F
(*b*) 0°-50°C
(*c*) 0°-100°F
(*d*) 10°-90°C.

Q. 356. A bear which eats a black bass is functioning as a

(*a*) primary consumer
(*b*) secondary consumer
(*c*) tertiary consumer
(*d*) key industry animal.

Q. 357. The deep part of the ocean from about 100 meters down to about 2000 meters is called

(*a*) abyssal zone
(*b*) oceanic zone
(*c*) neritic zone
(*d*) bathyal zone.

Q. 358. During the period of a population's maximum growth, the increase in the population is proportional to

(*a*) the food supply
(*b*) the number of individuals in the population
(*c*) the birth rate
(*d*) the death rate.

Q. 359. The primary oxygen-carrying mechanism in the blood of the earthworm consists of

(*a*) red cells
(*b*) blue cells

(c) dissolved hemoglobin
(d) haemocyanin.

Q. 360. The cellular layers of the earthworm are arranged in the following order:

(a) epidermis, circular muscle, longitudinal muscle, visceral peritoneum, parietal peritoneum, submucosa, epithelium
(b) epidermis, circular muscle, longitudinal muscle, parietal peritoneum, visceral peritoneum, submucosa, epithelium
(c) epidermis, longitudinal muscle, circular muscle, parietal peritoneum, visceral peritoneum, submucosa, epithelium
(d) epidermis, longitudinal muscle, circular muscle, chloragen layer, parietal peritoneum, submucosa, epithelium.

Q. 361. What biological significance is associated with the pronounced segmentation found in the annelids?

(a) evolutionary versatility in giving rise to new structures
(b) facilitation of reproduction each segment is literally a bag of eggs
(c) facilitation of burrowing through increased body flexibility
(d) increased longevity–the older tail segments are continuously being shed and replaced by newer ones.

Q. 362. There are cells lying between sperm-forming cells and which produce a hormone called

(a) estradiol
(b) testosterone
(c) progesterone
(d) aldosterone.

Q. 363. The primary result of secretion of estradiol (an estrogen) from the ovarian follicle is

(a) induces menstruation
(b) induces corpus luteum formation

(*c*) induces initial uterine thickening
(*d*) induces secondary uterine vascularization.

Q. 364. In terms of species numbers, the smallest vertebrate group at present is the class

(*a*) Amphibia
(*b*) Chondrichthyes
(*c*) Agnatha
(*d*) Osteichthes.

Q. 365. A cloaca is present in a

(*a*) shark
(*b*) chimera
(*c*) teleost
(*d*) lung-fish

Q. 366. Spawning in freshwater is characteristic of

(*a*) all lampreys
(*b*) only those lampreys living in freshwater
(*c*) only those lampreys in which the ammocoetes are marine
(*d*) none of the lampreys but all of the hagfishes.

Q. 367. In sharks, the spiral valve is

(*a*) a ventricular flap separating arterial and venous blood to some extent
(*b*) an opercular cover over the spiracles
(*c*) a clasping structure on the pelvic fins of males
(*d*) analogous to the typhlosole of earthworms.

Q. 368. The upper jaws are fused directly to the skull in

(*a*) sharks
(*b*) teleosts
(*c*) chimeras
(*d*) lampreys.

Q. 369. The original function of the ancestral vertebrate kidney probably was to

(*a*) eliminate excess salts
(*b*) eliminate excess water

(*c*) retain water but not salts
(*d*) retain both water and salts.

Q. 370. A lamprey possesses

(*a*) small dermal denticles
(*b*) no notochord in the adult stage
(*c*) a lateral line system
(*d*) a stomach.

Q. 371. Placoderms did not possess

(*a*) true teeth
(*b*) spiracles
(*c*) pelvic fins
(*d*) notochords as adults.

Q. 372. Paired fins with broad-base attachment are characteristic of

(*a*) all Actinopterygii
(*b*) Chondrostei
(*c*) Holostei
(*d*) Teleostei.

Q. 373. The density gradient centrifugation experiments gave results

(*a*) that were consistent with the Watson-Crick proposal for replication of DNA
(*b*) that could not be interpreted
(*c*) that indicated that DNA breaks up into many independent units before replication
(*d*) which indicated that the strands of DNA do not separate in replication but serve as a template for another double stranded molecule.

Q. 374. The product of the reaction catalyzed by DNA polymerase

(*a*) is a random polymer
(*b*) is the same no matter what primer is used
(*c*) reflects the base composition of the primer
(*d*) is usually formed in absence of a primer.

Q. 375. In an allelic pair of genes controlling a single character

(*a*) both genes come from the father

(*b*) both genes come from the mother
(*c*) one gene comes from the father and from the mother
(*d*) the genes come randomly from either father or mother.

Q. 376. In the offspring of the cross *AaBb* X *AaBb*

(*a*) kinds of genotypes will outnumber kinds of phenotypes
(*b*) kinds of phenotypes will outnumber kinds of genotypes
(*c*) kinds of genotypes and phenotypes will occur in equal numbers
(*d*) genotypes will occur in a 9:3:3:1 ratio.

Q. 377. Natural mutations occur with a frequency of about one in every

(*a*) 100 cells
(*b*) 1,000 cells
(*c*) 1 million cells
(*d*) 1 billion cells.

Q. 378. An offspring generally inherits

(*a*) all mutations
(*b*) only somatic mutations
(*c*) only germ mutations
(*d*) only dominant mutations.

Q. 379. If *A* as well as *B* can produce red color, a cross *AaBb* X *AaBb* will yield

(*a*) 3
(*b*) 9
(*c*) 12
(*d*) 15, red offspring out of every 16.

Q. 380. If two pairs of genes are located on the same chromosome pair, and crossing-over occurs, the gametes which are formed will be of

(*a*) one
(*b*) two
(*c*) four
(*d*) eight, different types.

Q. 381. In an animal in which the haploid chromosome number is two, each gamete will contain

(*a*) eight
(*b*) four
(*c*) two
(*d*) one, chromosome(s).

Q. 382. Most mutations have no immediate effect because

(*a*) they occur so rarely
(*b*) they are largely recessive
(*c*) they are largely lethal
(*d*) they affect only one cell at a time.

Q. 383. If *A* is essential for the production of skin pigment and the recessive factor *b* prevents skin color when present in the homozygous state, than an individual with the genotype

(*a*) *AaBb*
(*b*) *AAbb*
(*c*) *AABb*
(*d*) *AaBB*, would be an albino.

Q. 384. A human female can produce

(*a*) 2^{46}
(*b*) 46^2
(*c*) 23^2
(*d*) 2^{23}, genetically different types of eggs.

Q. 385. In the worm *Bonellia*, sex determination takes place in the

(*a*) zygote state
(*b*) embryonic stage
(*c*) larval stage
(*d*) adult stage.

Q. 386. All mollusks possess a radula except the

(*a*) scaphopods
(*b*) monoplacophorans
(*c*) pelecypods
(*d*) gastropods.

Q. 387. A crystalline style is particularly important in the digestive activity of

(*a*) scaphopods
(*b*) monoplacophorans
(*c*) pelecypods
(*d*) gastropods.

Q. 388. Structures called captacula are found in

(*a*) scaphopods
(*b*) monoplacophorans
(*c*) pelecypods
(*d*) gastropods.

Q. 389. Glochindia larvae are found in some

(*a*) scaphopods
(*b*) monoplacophorans
(*c*) pelecypods
(*d*) gastropods.

Q. 390. Sperm in the frog pass from the testes through the following structures in order

(*a*) mesonephric tubules, mesonephric duct, vasa efferentia, cloaca
(*b*) mesonephric duct, mesonephric tubules, vasa efferentia, cloaca
(*c*) vasa efferentia, mesonephric duct, mesonephric tubules, cloaca
(*d*) vasa efferentia, mesonephric tubules, mesonephric duct, cloaca.

Q. 391. The hormone FSH

(*a*) is produced by the pituitary and acts directly on the ovary
(*b*) is produced in the ovary and acts directly on the pituitary
(*c*) is produced in the ovary and acts directly on the uterus
(*d*) is produced in the pituitary and acts directly on the uterus.

Q. 392. The structure in the human male derived from the homologue of the frog's kidney in part is

(*a*) testis
(*b*) Cowper's gland
(*c*) prostate gland
(*d*) epididymis.

Q. 393. The structure which develops in the ovary immediately after ovulation is

(*a*) the Graafian follicle under FSH stimulus
(*b*) the corpus luteum under FSH stimulus
(*c*) the Graafian follicle under LH stimulus
(*d*) the corpus luteum under LH stimulus.

Q. 394. Cyprinoids, such as goldfishes and minnows, are characterized by

(*a*) Weberian ossicles
(*b*) swim bladders without ducts
(*c*) ctenoid scales
(*d*) heterocercal tails.

Q. 395. Bony fishes possess

(*a*) a cloaca
(*b*) separate excretory, reproductive, and alimentary exits
(*c*) urogenital sinus in both sexes
(*d*) a urogenital sinus in males but separate urinary and reproductive openings in females.

Q. 396. Sarcopterygii are represented today by

(*a*) the coelacanths only
(*b*) three genera of lungfishes only
(*c*) four genera only
(*d*) primitive fishes with spiracles, e.g., strugeons, garpikes, and some other types.

Q. 397. In primitive teleosts

(*a*) spiracles are present
(*b*) the tail is homocercal
(*c*) paired fins have broad-base attachment
(*d*) swim bladders are without ducts.

Q. 398. The superclass Pisces comprises

(*a*) all aquatic vertebrates
(*b*) only amniotes
(*c*) all anamniotes
(*d*) only poikilothermic types.

Q. 399. A couple whose blood types are A and B may have a child with which of the following blood types?

(*a*) AB only
(*b*) A, B only
(*c*) A, B, O only
(*d*) A, B, AB and O.

Q. 400. Which enzyme is not produced by the pancreas?

(*a*) amylase
(*b*) carboxypeptidase
(*c*) aminopeptidase
(*d*) lipase.

Section V

Q. 401. In the frog, which of these structures does not function in digestion?

(*a*) duodenum
(*b*) salivary glands
(*c*) stomach
(*d*) pancreas.

Q. 402. Besides its digestive functions, the liver serves as an organ of storage. Which is not a compound stored in the liver?

(*a*) vitamin A
(*b*) calcium salts for the repair of bone and cartilage
(*c*) glycogen
(*d*) iron from worn out blood cells.

Q. 403. The study of animals suggests that the evolution of new types has occurred as a

(*a*) branching progression
(*b*) essentially chaotic progression
(*c*) straight-line progression
(*d*) goal-seeking progression.

Q. 404. It is now fairly well established that acquired characteristics

(*a*) can never be inherited
(*b*) can always be inherited
(*c*) can be inherited in certain special cases
(*d*) play a major role in evolution.

Q. 405. Darwin's theory of natural selection

(*a*) was the first theory of evolution
(*b*) failed to explain the source of variability
(*c*) has been replaced completely
(*d*) did not account for fossils.

Q. 406. If correct, Lamarck's theory of evolution would imply that

(*a*) genes are influenced by what an organism does
(*b*) an organism is influenced by what its genes do
(*c*) organisms are unable to influence their genes
(*d*) genes are unable to influence the organisms in which they occur.

Q. 407. The concept of organic evolution implies

(*a*) purposeful change in animals
(*b*) random survival of animals
(*c*) struggle for survival
(*d*) survival of the best reproducers.

Q. 408. Lamarck's theory of evolution

(*a*) was based on natural selection
(*b*) did not account for fossils
(*c*) claimed that heredity could be modified
(*d*) claimed that the giraffe had a long neck.

Q. 409. Attachment by means of byssus threads is common among

(*a*) scaphopods
(*b*) monoplacophorans
(*c*) pelecypods
(*d*) gastropods.

Q. 410. Which of the following are hermaphroditic?

(*a*) cephalopods
(*b*) freshwater claims

(*c*) pulmonate snails
(*d*) scaphopods.

Q. 411. Pearls are secreted by the

(*a*) crystalline style
(*b*) edge of the mantle
(*c*) inner surface of the mantle
(*d*) outer surface of the mantle.

Q. 412. The dart sac is

(*a*) a protective device found in *Dentalium*
(*b*) a protective device found in *Neopilina*
(*c*) associated with mating in some snails
(*d*) a modified radula.

Q. 413. The molluscan coelom is

(*a*) well-developed
(*b*) greatly reduced
(*c*) an enterocoel
(*d*) restricted to the mantle cavity.

Q. 414. Which of the following is found in *Gonionemus* but not in *Hydra?*

(*a*) basal disc
(*b*) hypostome
(*c*) tentacles
(*d*) radial canal.

Q. 415. Coelenterata of the class Hydrozoa are distinguished from the sponges in which one of the following respects?

(*a*) Hydrozoa possesses two body layer–the endoderm and ectoderm
(*b*) Sponges are multicellular organisms
(*c*) Hydrozoa are often sessile
(*d*) Hydrozoa obtain food that is floating in water.

Q. 416. *Hydra* reproduces asexually by means of

(*a*) gametes
(*b*) gonads
(*c*) nematocysts
(*d*) budding.

Q. 417. Which of the following is found in both hydra and the earthworm?

(*a*) ectoderm
(*b*) metameres
(*c*) gastrovascular cavity
(*d*) coelom.

Q. 418. Among vertebrates, truly viviparous types occur

(*a*) in mammals only
(*b*) in all tetrapod classes except birds
(*c*) in amphibia, reptiles, and mammals but in not other classes
(*d*) in all gnathostome classes.

Q. 419. Among living amphibia, fertilization is internal only in

(*a*) cecilians
(*b*) terrestrial urodeles
(*c*) terrestrial anurans
(*d*) certain tree frogs.

Q. 420. Toads have teeth on

(*a*) both jaws
(*b*) upper jaw only
(*c*) lower jaw only
(*d*) neither jaw.

Q. 421. Frogs have teeth on

(*a*) both jaws
(*b*) upper jaw only
(*c*) lower jaw only
(*d*) neither jaw.

Q. 422. The number of aortic arches in the larvae of terrestrial amphibia is

(*a*) one
(*b*) three
(*c*) four
(*d*) six.

Q. 423. Mudpuppies are among amphibia which possess

(*a*) gills and lungs
(*b*) gills only
(*c*) lungs only
(*d*) gills only during the larval, and lungs only during the adult, stage.

Q. 424. According to Darwin

(*a*) acquired characteristics are not inherited
(*b*) adapted animals survive best
(*c*) the unfit have no right to survive
(*d*) men descended from gorillas.

Q. 425. The modern theory of evolution was formulated by

(*a*) Darwin and Wallace
(*b*) Darwin and Mendel
(*c*) Hardy and Weinberg
(*d*) synthesis of the work of numerous zoologists.

Q. 426. Lamarck's theory of evolution

(*a*) was based on the inheritance of acquired characters
(*b*) claimed heredity could not be modified
(*c*) said fossils were the result of the great deluge
(*d*) rejected the notion of use and disuse.

Q. 427. The Lamarckian interpretation of the appearance of webbed feet in ducks would involve

(*a*) stretching of the skin between the toes as a result of continued life in water
(*b*) development of webbing as a result of mutation
(*c*) survival of forms with webbing in an aquatic habitat
(*d*) recognition by ducks that webbed feet would be advantageous.

Q. 428. Extinction in evolution

(*a*) is inherently unavoidable
(*b*) gives rise to new types by adaptive radiation
(*c*) occurs universally on the species level
(*d*) occurs very frequently on the phylum level.

Q. 429. In the absence of selective forces and mutations, the frequency of any given gene in a large population will

(a) remain the same indefinitely
(b) change slowly in some unpredictable direction
(c) change slowly and predictably
(d) always decrease, because of replacement.

Q. 430. During the history of the earth

(a) no new forms have arisen
(b) life has tended to increase in variety
(c) extinction of major groups has been the rule
(d) rates of evolution have increased steadily.

Q. 431. One of the most frequent sources of variation in animals is

(a) the establishment of new combinations of genes already in existence
(b) vegetative propagation of existing types
(c) continued use of structures, making them more efficient
(d) the appearance of reproductive barriers.

Q. 432. Recessive mutations can become homozygous in nature because

(a) dominants are selected against.
(b) recessives are selected for
(c) breeding does not take place at random
(d) they are more common there.

Q. 433. A couple has five offspring, all females. What is the probability that the next child will be a girl?

(a) 1/6
(b) $(1/2)^6$
(c) $(1/2)^5$
(d) ½

Q. 434. The cross between a yellow male and a tortoise-sheel female cat results in which phenotypic ratio?

(a) all yellow
(b) yellow females, black males
(c) 2 yellow females, 1 yellow male, 1 tortoise male
(d) 1 yellow male, 1 black male, 1 yellow female, 1 tortoise female.

Q. 435. Most somatic cells of a species

(*a*) contain the same amount of DNA
(*b*) contain the same amount of RNA
(*c*) contain the same amount of protein
(*d*) contain twice as much protein as DNA.

Q. 436. Gametes contain about

(*a*) twice as much DNA as protein
(*b*) twice as much DNA as do the somatic cells
(*c*) one half as much DNA as do the somatic cells
(*d*) one half as much RNA as do the somatic cells.

Q. 437. The action spectrum of UV-induced mutagenesis is

(*a*) similar to the absorption spectrum for hemoglobin
(*b*) similar to the absorption spectrum for proteins
(*c*) similar to the absorption spectrum for nucleic acids
(*d*) insignificant in deciding the nature of the genetic material.

Q. 438. Lorenz has shown that behavior patterns

(*a*) are not capable of evolution
(*b*) have no use in phylogenetic studies
(*c*) may change slowly as organisms evolve
(*d*) are all species specific.

Q. 439. The hypothalamus is the region of the brain particularly involved in

(*a*) memory
(*b*) classical conditioning
(*c*) regulation of drives
(*d*) circadian rhythms.

Q. 440. The interval of time called the critical period is important to the behavior classified as

(*a*) habituation
(*b*) operant conditioning
(*c*) reflex
(*d*) imprinting.

Q. 441. Echiurids possess

(*a*) a retractable proboscis
(*b*) special cells called urn cells which are believed to function in excretion
(*c*) a closed circulatory system
(*d*) no setae.

Q. 442. Members of the phylum Echiurida

(*a*) are monoecious
(*b*) live in fresh and salt waters
(*c*) always have a pair of setae on the anterior ventral surface
(*d*) have an anteriorly located anus.

Q. 443. In colonial forms like *Obelia*, the upright portion which bears the polyps is called

(*a*) perisarc
(*b*) hydrotheca
(*c*) coenosarc
(*d*) hydrocaulus.

Q. 444. The phylum Coelenterata includes

(*a*) sponges
(*b*) jellyfishes
(*c*) ascaris
(*d*) tapeworms.

Q. 445. Corals belong to the phylum

(*a*) Porifera
(*b*) Protozoa
(*c*) Coelenterata
(*d*) Aschelminthes.

Q. 446. Which of the following constitutes the main defense mechanism of hydra?

(*a*) trichocysts
(*b*) blastocysts
(*c*) rhabdites
(*d*) nematocysts.

Q. 447. Man can control the pattern of evolution by

(*a*) modifying genes
(*b*) modifying the environment
(*c*) providing an environment essential to the expression of new gene combinations
(*d*) no known means, if stable new species are wanted.

Q. 448. The Hardy-Weinberg law implies that evolution cannot occur unless

(*a*) a population is large
(*b*) genetic drift is ruled out
(*c*) gene frequencies change
(*d*) mating is random.

Q. 449. Gene frequencies in a population will remain constant only if

(*a*) the population is large and mating is nonrandom
(*b*) mating is random and mutations do not occur
(*c*) the population is small and mutations do occur
(*d*) the population is large and the mutation-rate is constant.

Q. 450. The meaning of natural selection is best expressed by the phrase

(*a*) survival of the fittest
(*b*) inheritance of adaptive traits
(*c*) the speed of evolution is proportional to population size
(*d*) differential reproduction.

Q. 451. Nonadaptive trends in evolution

(*a*) could occur in small populations
(*b*) are common generally
(*c*) are not gene-determined
(*d*) have been proved to be inherently impossible.

Q. 452. "Living fossils"

(*a*) are not really fossils because they are alive
(*b*) are not really living, but are fossils resembling living forms greatly
(*c*) show that rates of evolution are surprisingly constant for most groups
(*d*) is a phrase synonymous with "hopeful monsters".

Q. 453. Evolution on the level of species or below

(*a*) can be made to occur in the laboratory
(*b*) occurs through a mechanism different from that of macroevolution
(*c*) is what the hypothesis of hopeful monsters aims to explain
(*d*) plays little role in evolution in nature.

Q. 454. The two heart ventricles are fully separated in

(*a*) all reptiles
(*b*) all reptiles except the turtles
(*c*) crocodiles
(*d*) none of the living reptiles.

Q. 455. Snakes do, but lizards do not, have

(*a*) external ear openings
(*b*) urinary bladders
(*c*) unmovable eyelids
(*d*) horny epidermal scales.

Q. 456. Color vision is now known to characterize

(*a*) turtles
(*b*) birds, crocodiles
(*c*) crocodiles
(*d*) lizards.

Q. 457. When their mouth is closed, alligators are distinguishable from other Crocodilia by their

(*a*) narrow jaws and exposed fourth pair of teeth
(*b*) broad jaws and exposed fourth pair of teeth
(*c*) narrow jaws and absence of exposed teeth
(*d*) broad jaws and absence of exposed teeth.

Q. 458. The oviparity of birds is probably correlated directly with the

(*a*) shelled nature of the eggs
(*b*) absence of external genitalia
(*c*) requirement of internal fertilization
(*d*) weight limitation of flight.

Q. 459. Most species of birds are

(*a*) colorblind
(*b*) passerine
(*c*) four-fingered
(*d*) ratite.

Q. 460. In the process of landing, a bird is likely to make most direct use of its

(*a*) sclerotic plates
(*b*) alulae
(*c*) uropygial glands
(*d*) nictitating membranes.

Q. 461. Squirrels are without

(*a*) incisors
(*b*) canines
(*c*) premolars
(*d*) molars.

Q. 462. Elephant tusks are elongated

(*a*) incisors
(*b*) canines
(*c*) premolars
(*d*) molars.

Q. 463. Most of the teeth in a human adult are

(*a*) incisors
(*b*) canines
(*c*) premolars
(*d*) molars.

Q. 464. Egg-laying mammals comprise the taxonomic category

(*a*) Theria
(*b*) Prototheria
(*c*) Metatheria
(*d*) Eutheria.

Q. 465. Separate urinary and reproductive orifices are characteristic of

(*a*) all mammalian males
(*b*) all monotreme females

(*c*) all marsupial males
(*d*) all placental females.

Q. 466. Although hermaphroditism is common in flatworms generally, the sexes are separate in

(*a*) *Dugesia*
(*b*) *Schistosoma*
(*c*) *Fasciola*
(*d*) *Taenia.*

Q. 467. The excretory system in the phylum Rhynchocoela

(*a*) is absent
(*b*) contains protonephridial flame bulbs
(*c*) is accomplished via the Rhynchocoel in some genera
(*d*) is accomplished by cell rosettes.

Q. 468. Examination of the reproductive system of a typical member of the phylum Rhynchocoela reveals

(*a*) both ovaries and testes in one individual arranged in a linear fashion between diverticulae of the intestine
(*b*) either ovaries or testes in any one individual arranged in a linear fashion between diverticulae of the intestine
(*c*) a long coiled oviduct or vas deferens which opens into the posterior portion of the intestine
(*d*) a long coiled oviduct which opens by its own pore in the middle of the animal or a long coiled vas deferens which opens into a cloaca.

Q. 469. The larval form characteristic of the phylum Rhynchocoela is the

(*a*) planula
(*b*) amphiblastula
(*c*) pilidium
(*d*) miricidium.

Q. 470. *Ascaris* infection of man occurs

(*a*) by eating infected pork
(*b*) by eating infected beef
(*c*) by eating food contaminated with fecal matter containing *Ascaris* eggs

(*d*) by entry into the skin, commonly through the sole of the foot when a barefooted individual steps on a larva.

Q. 471. Excretion in the class Nematoda is accomplished by

(*a*) unicellular flame cells
(*b*) multicellular flame cells
(*c*) simple diffusion through the body wall
(*d*) excretory tubules in the lateral line.

Q. 472. The roundworms

(*a*) have a mouth, and gastrovascular cavity
(*b*) have a mouth, anus and coelom
(*c*) have a mouth, anus and pseudocoel
(*d*) have a mouth, anus, pseudocoel and flame cells.

Q. 473. The method whereby *Wuchereria* enters its host is through

(*a*) the mouth
(*b*) cuts and wounds
(*c*) active larval penetration of the skin
(*d*) introduction into the blood by mosquitoes.

Q. 474. Water is biologically vital because it

(*a*) is nontoxic
(*b*) has low density
(*c*) dissolves many substances
(*d*) is found everywhere.

Q. 475. The earliest living organisms must have had the capacity to

(*a*) live in fresh water
(*b*) live at high temperatures
(*c*) utilize the energy stored in various chemicals
(*d*) photosynthesize.

Q. 476. Viruses resemble living organisms in that they

(*a*) can move
(*b*) contain a nucleus
(*c*) can mutate
(*d*) are cellular in structure.

Q. 477. During the origin of life, reproductive capacity probably was exhibited first by

(*a*) early cells
(*b*) early proteins
(*c*) early nucleic acids
(*d*) early nucleotides.

Q. 478. Which of the following is a mismatch?

(*a*) von Frisch–honey bee communication
(*b*) W.G. Vanderkloot–process of cocoon spinning
(*c*) Lorenz–operant conditioning
(*d*) Karl Lashley–memory in rats.

Q. 479. Which is not true of the reflex?

(*a*) involves the spinal chord
(*b*) automatic
(*c*) unlearned
(*d*) does not occur if the brain is destroyed.

Q. 480. Maturation is involved in

(*a*) remembering
(*b*) conditioning
(*c*) walking of newly born rats
(*d*) mating of *Drosophila*.

Q. 481. All of the following are involved in cocoon spinning of the cecropia moth caterpillar except

(*a*) "mushroom bodies"
(*b*) orientation by gravity
(*c*) hormones
(*d*) memory.

Q. 482. The sipunculids

(*a*) are segmented as larvae but not as adults
(*b*) are not segmented at any stage in their life cycle
(*c*) have an open circulatory system
(*d*) are monoccious.

Q. 483. In members of the phylum Sipunculida

(*a*) excretion is by protonephridial flame cells

(*b*) excretion is by a pair of metanephridia
(*c*) there is no larval stage
(*d*) the coelom is an enterocoel.

Q. 484. Select the series which has only the parts of the female reproductive system of *Planaria*:

(*a*) seminal receptacles, flame cells, seminal vesicles, ovary, oviducts
(*b*) ovary, oviducts, seminal receptacles, yolk glands
(*c*) oviducts, seminal vesicles, ovary, yolk glands
(*d*) oviducts, seminal receptacles, ovary, vas deferens.

Q. 485. *Planaria* differs from the coelenterates in the following ways:

(*a*) It possesses nematocysts, has a gastrovascular cavity, and has no sense organs
(*b*) It has a gastrovascular cavity, principally epithelio-muscular cells for locomotion and is sessile
(*c*) It has a gastrovascular cavity, flame cells and nematocysts
(*d*) It has flame cells, has a ladder type nervous system, and is not sessile.

Q. 486. Females of egg-laying mammals

(*a*) do not produce milk
(*b*) are without a cloaca
(*c*) are without nipples
(*d*) lay unshelled eggs.

Q. 487. The lowest taxonomic rank which embraces both dogs and wolves is that of

(*a*) species
(*b*) genus
(*c*) family
(*d*) suborder.

Q. 488. In members of the phylum Acanthocephala

(*a*) mouth and intestine are present but there is no anus
(*b*) the digestive system is reduced to a rudimentary mouth

(c) the sexes are separate
(d) the life cycle always includes a snail as an intermediate host.

Q. 489. In the class Rotifera males

(a) are larger than females
(b) are found all year around
(c) develop from small unfertilized eggs
(d) do not occur.

Q. 490. Members of the class Gastrotricha are

(a) exclusively marine
(b) without means of locomotion in the adult stage
(c) hermaphroditic
(d) provided with a well-developed circulatory system.

Q. 491. Members of the class Kinorhyncha

(a) have a non-retractable anterior end
(b) are deep-sea dwellers
(c) have thickenings in the hypodermis similar to those in the nematodes
(d) have no excretory system.

Q. 492. The priapulids

(a) are clearly members of the phylum Aschelminthes because the anterior end resembles that of a hookworm
(b) have highly coiled and u-shaped intestines
(c) have a protonephridial excretory system with solenocytes
(d) have segmentally arranged muscles.

Q. 493. Chemosynthesizers and photosynthesizers have in common that they

(a) require light
(b) possess chlorophyll
(c) manufacture food
(d) are all bacteria.

Q. 494. Parasites and saprotrophs have in common that they

(a) are infective

(*b*) subsist on living hosts
(*c*) are harmful to their hosts
(*d*) do not create foods.

Q. 495. Aerobic respiration could not have occurred

(*a*) after the oxygen-revolution
(*b*) before the evolution of photosynthesis
(*c*) after the disappearance of free foods from the early oceans
(*d*) before the evolution of true animals.

Q. 496. It is most likely that the first cell-like structures arose

(*a*) in the open ocean
(*b*) in the early atmosphere
(*c*) along the sea shore
(*d*) about 2 million years ago.

Q. 497. Organisms like *Euglena* are

(*a*) altogether plant-like
(*b*) altogether animal-like
(*c*) both plant–and animal-like
(*d*) neither plant-nor animal-like.

Q. 498. The embryos of frogs and man develop similarly for a relatively longer period than do the embryos of

(*a*) lizard and man
(*b*) fish and man
(*c*) bird and man
(*d*) monkey and man.

Q. 499. Human embryos

(*a*) never exhibit gill-like structures during their development
(*b*) possess nonfunctional, rudimentary gills at one stage of development
(*c*) possess functional gills at one stage of development
(*d*) possess structurally complete but nonfunctional gills at one stage of development.

Q. 500. Of the animals listed, man is most closely related to

(*a*) flatworms
(*b*) earthworms
(*c*) social insects
(*d*) startfish.

Section VI

Q. 501. According to the currently most widely accepted views, the first Eumetazoa probably were

(*a*) ciliate protozoa
(*b*) sponges
(*c*) coelenterates
(*d*) flatworms.

Q. 502. Haeckel's views are not accepted today in part because

(*a*) ontogeny clearly recapitualtes phylogeny
(*b*) germ layers have no real embryological meaning
(*c*) most Eumetazoa are triploblastic
(*d*) invaginative gastrulation is exceptionally rare among animals.

Q. 503. Evolution by embryonic end-additions

(*a*) appears to have occurred among vertebrates
(*b*) has been virtually nonexistent
(*c*) is the general rule in animal evolution
(*d*) lies at the root of the bush pattern of animal evolution.

Q. 504. Ethologists are particularly concerned with

(*a*) instincts and behavioral adptations
(*b*) neurophysiology
(*c*) mechanisms of adaptations
(*d*) the nature of learning.

Q. 505. Male *Aedes* mosquitoes will fly to a tuning fork which emits a sound similar in pitch to that made by the female mosquito. The illustrates

(*a*) learned response
(*b*) releasing stimulus
(*c*) operant conditioning
(*d*) taxis.

Q. 506. Pheromones are not

(*a*) important to the behavior of social insects
(*b*) chemical substances that affect behavior
(*c*) secreted by many organisms
(*d*) primarily involved in learned behavior.

Q. 507. Honey bees

(*a*) are not capable of learning
(*b*) use polarized light from the sun for orientation
(*c*) communicate the direction of a distant food source by means of the round dance
(*d*) are not capable of finding food on cloudy days.

Q. 508. Which of the following is true?

(*a*) no mollusks are segmented
(*b*) a primitive form of mollusk is segmented
(*c*) all mollusks are segmented
(*d*) segmentation is not pertinent to the study of phylogeny.

Q. 509. The cephalopod eye

(*a*) is similar to the vertebrate eye
(*b*) is similar to the planarian eye
(*c*) is a compound eye
(*d*) is evidence for common ancestry of vertebrates and mollusks.

Q. 510. The most primitive mollusks are probably the

(*a*) scaphopods
(*b*) monoplacophorans
(*c*) pelecypods
(*d*) gastropods.

Q. 511. The class Trematoda

(*a*) includes all of the parasites
(*b*) includes all of the flukes
(*c*) includes all non-parasitic flukes
(*d*) includes the tapeworms.

Q. 512. The unit of excretory function in planarians is

(*a*) the flame cell

(*b*) the nephridium
(*c*) the uriniferous tubule
(*d*) the loop of Henle.

Q. 513 Muller's larva is characteristic of

(*a*) acoels
(*b*) rhabdocoels
(*c*) triclads
(*d*) polyclads.

Q. 514. A micricidium larva of the flukes is

(*a*) tailed but unciliated
(*b*) untailed but ciliated
(*c*) tailed and ciliated
(*d*) untailed and unciliated.

Q. 515. Stanley Miller's experiment concerning the origin of life did not include which of the following?

(*a*) water
(*b*) methane
(*c*) glucose
(*d*) hydrogen.

Q. 516. Which one of the following does not change the frequency of genes in a population?

(*a*) mutation
(*b*) selection
(*c*) migration
(*d*) asexual reproduction.

Q. 517. Mutations are generally

(*a*) dominant, random, deleterious
(*b*) dominant, random, beneficial
(*c*) recessive, random, deleterious
(*d*) recessive, random, beneficial.

Q. 518. Digestion in *Planaria* is mainly

(*a*) intracellular, in the cytoplasm proper
(*b*) extracellular
(*c*) intracellular, in food vacuoles of the cytoplasm
(*d*) intracellular, in the mitochondria.

Q. 519. Coordination in *Planaria* is accomplished by

(*a*) a ladder type nervous system
(*b*) a diffuse nervous system similar to that of the coelenterates
(*c*) diffusion of neurohumors from one cell to another; no easily recognizable system is present
(*d*) a dorsal nerve cord.

Q. 520. *Planaria* reproduce

(*a*) asexually by fission
(*b*) asexually by fragmentation
(*c*) asexually by fission and fragmentation
(*d*) asexually by fission and sexually.

Q. 521. The regeneration of planarian tissue as explained by C.M. Child

(*a*) involves an antero-posterior gradient of a physiological nature
(*b*) involves a postero-anterior gradient of a physiological nature
(*c*) involves disaggregation of tissues into a disorganized cellular mass followed by reaggregation into organized individuals
(*d*) increases with organizational specialization.

Q. 522. According to widely held current hypotheses

(*a*) the first coelom-possessing animals were schizocoelic
(*b*) the animal coelom evolved twice
(*c*) metamerism evolved twice
(*d*) the annelid and vertebrate body plans are mirror-images of each other.

Q. 523. The most primitive coelomate animals probably include the

(*a*) lophophorates
(*b*) segmented schizocoelomates
(*c*) unsegmented schiozocoelomates
(*d*) deuterostomes.

Q. 524. Cellular absorption of glucose is accomplished by

(*a*) cyclosis
(*b*) osmosis
(*c*) phosphorylation
(*d*) diffusion.

Q. 525. Fermentation is

(*a*) the production of alcohol
(*b*) the breakdown of sugar in the absence of oxygen
(*c*) aerobic respiration
(*d*) energy-production by bacteria and yeasts.

Q. 526. The steps involved in the conversion of carbohydrates to C_3 compounds are

(*a*) common to both aerobic and anaerobic respiration
(*b*) occur only in aerobic respiration
(*c*) occur only in anaerobic respiration
(*d*) occur only in the citric acid cycle.

Q. 527. ATP is a

(*a*) respiratory enzyme
(*b*) energy acceptor
(*c*) hydrogen carrier
(*d*) phosphate donor.

Q. 528. In the citric acid cycle

(*a*) pyruvic acid is formed
(*b*) carbon dioxide is formed
(*c*) DPN or TPN is formed
(*d*) acetyl CoA is formed.

Q. 529. Respiratory enzymes within a cell are concentrated largely in the

(*a*) chromosomes
(*b*) microsomes
(*c*) endoplasmic reticulum
(*d*) mitochondria.

Q. 530. FAD passes hydrogen to

(*a*) pyruvic acid in anaerobic respiration
(*b*) oxygen

(*c*) the cytochromes
(*d*) DPN.

Q. 531. The first observable fact which Darwin used in postulating his theory was that

(*a*) there is not a realization of reproductive potential
(*b*) there is individual variation within species
(*c*) every species tends to increase geometrically
(*d*) mutations tend to be lethal.

Q. 532. In modern evolutionary thinking the most significant unit is the

(*a*) nucleotide
(*b*) gene
(*c*) chromosome
(*d*) population.

Q. 533. In members of the phylum Phoronida, the coelom

(*a*) is a schizocoel
(*b*) is an enterocoel
(*c*) develops from mesenchyme cells which form a hollow sac
(*d*) is obliterated in the adult.

Q. 534. In members of the phylum Ectoprocta the coelom

(*a*) is a schizocoel
(*b*) is an enterocoel
(*c*) is obliterated in the adult
(*d*) arise from larval ectoderm cells.

Q. 535. In members of the class Articulata of the phylum Brachiopoda the coelom

(*a*) is a schizocoel
(*b*) is an enterocoel
(*c*) arise from larval ectoderm cells
(*d*) develops from mesenchyme cells which form a hollow sac.

Q. 536. Which of the following shows alteration of generations?

(*a*) crayfish

(*b*) planaria
(*c*) *Obelia*
(*d*) earthworm.

Q. 537. The basic larval form characteristic of the entire phylum Coelenterata is

(*a*) planula
(*b*) amphiblastula
(*c*) pilidium
(*d*) miricidium.

Q. 538. The sea anemones and corals belong to the class

(*a*) Anthozoa
(*b*) Scyphozoa
(*c*) Metazoa
(*d*) Hydrozoa.

Q. 539. The coelenterate stinging cell is

(*a*) a nematocyst
(*b*) a cnidocil
(*c*) a cnidoblast
(*d*) a mesogleal cell.

Q. 540. A distinguishing characteristic of the coelenterata is

(*a*) nematocysts
(*b*) reproduction by budding
(*c*) a gastrovascular cavity
(*d*) exchange of gases with the environment by diffusion.

Q. 541. Dinosaurs thrived during the

(*a*) Cambrian
(*b*) Devonian
(*c*) Cretaceous
(*d*) Miocene.

Q. 542. Most of today's coal deposits were formed during the

(*a*) Carboniferous
(*b*) Cambrian
(*c*) Cenozoic
(*d*) Cretaceous.

Q. 543. Fossils first appear abundantly in the

(*a*) Precambrian
(*b*) Paleozoic
(*c*) Mesozoic
(*d*) Cenozoic.

Q. 544. Homo sapiens arose approximately

(*a*) 20,000 years ago
(*b*) 50,000 years ago
(*c*) 200,000 years ago
(*d*) 500,000 years ago.

Q. 545. The most complex type of body form in sponges is

(*a*) ascon
(*b*) leucon
(*c*) olynthus
(*d*) sycon.

Q. 546. Reproduction in lower organisms by the formation of a small replica of the parent as an outgrowth from the body of the parent is called

(*a*) budding
(*b*) binary fission
(*c*) mitosis
(*d*) amitosis.

Q. 547. Asexual reproduction in the sponges may take place by the formation of

(*a*) statocysts
(*b*) statoblasts
(*c*) spongioblasts
(*d*) gemmules.

Q. 548. Coal deposits indicate the past geological existence of

(*a*) inland oceans
(*b*) forest swamps
(*c*) ice ages
(*d*) trilobites.

Q. 549. The most complete series of fossil remains are known for

(*a*) horses
(*b*) man
(*c*) crustacea
(*d*) fishes.

Q. 550. The Mesozoic Era is often called the

(*a*) age of mammals
(*b*) age of fishes
(*c*) age of reptiles
(*d*) age of invertebrates.

Q. 551. The ancestors of primates were probably related to the

(*a*) Carnivora
(*b*) Herbivora
(*c*) Insectivora
(*d*) Omnivora.

Q. 552. Each major geologic Era closed with

(*a*) a period of extreme heat
(*b*) a period of extreme wetness
(*c*) a period of deep seas
(*d*) a period of mountain building.

Q. 553. Periods of mountain building in the earth's history caused large-scale extinction of animal groups because

(*a*) the oceans dried up
(*b*) animals were killed in earthquakes and volcanic eruptions
(*c*) new groups took over
(*d*) drastic climatic changes took place

Q. 554. A study of fossils suggests that the immediate ancestors of birds were prechistoric

(*a*) reptiles
(*b*) amphibia
(*c*) bony fishes
(*d*) cartilage fishes.

Q. 555. A study of fossils suggests that mammals have evolved directly from

(*a*) fishes
(*b*) amphibia
(*c*) reptiles
(*d*) birds.

Q. 556. Bony fishes acquired their present status of dominace

(*a*) during the Devonian, known as the age of fishes
(*b*) during the Cenozoic, known as the age of mammals
(*c*) during the Mesozoic, known as the age of reptiles
(*d*) at roughly the same time as sharks and other cartilage fishes.

Q. 557. The jawless fishes

(*a*) gave rise to the placoderms
(*b*) are now extinct
(*c*) evolved during the Precambrian
(*d*) were the direct ancestors of the lobefins and lungfishes.

Q. 558. The most primitive living primates are found in

(*a*) Java
(*b*) China
(*c*) Madagascar
(*d*) Australia.

Q. 559. The Mesozoic Era lasted approximately

(*a*) 50 million years
(*b*) 100 million years
(*c*) 150 million years
(*d*) 300 million years.

Q. 560. *Archeopteryx* was a

(*a*) mammal-like reptile
(*b*) bird-like mammal
(*c*) reptile-like bird
(*d*) dinosaur.

Q. 561. The first mammals lived in the

(*a*) Cenozoic

(*b*) Paleozoic
(*c*) Mesozoic
(*d*) Paleocene.

Q. 562. Major types, of phyla

(*a*) have not become extinct
(*b*) have become extinct in many cases
(*c*) have appeared in every geologic period during evolutionary history
(*d*) all arose at the time of the origin of life.

Q. 563. With respect to the following three statements (1) the labyrinthodonts gave rise to the reptiles, (2) therapsids were mammal-like reptiles, (3) insectivores belong to the class Aves, give the best answer:

(*a*) 1 and 2 are correct
(*b*) 1 and 3 are correct
(*c*) 2 and 3 are correct
(*d*) 1, 2 and 3 are correct.

Q. 564. The oldest known vertebrates were

(*a*) stegocephalians
(*b*) sharks
(*c*) ostrachoderms
(*d*) eurypterids.

Q. 565. *Homo erectus* appeared approximately

(*a*) 10-20 milllion years ago
(*b*) 500,000-600,000 years ago
(*c*) 1-2 million years ago
(*d*) 10-20,000 years ago.

Q. 566. In members of the phylum Phoronida developmental stages include

(*a*) a cyphonautes larva
(*b*) a cydippid larva
(*c*) an actinotroch larva
(*d*) a dipleurula larva.

Q. 567. In phoronids there is

(*a*) a well-developed open circulatory system
(*b*) a well-developed closed circulatory system
(*c*) no circulatory system
(*d*) a peculiar system of epidermal lacunae which serve as a circulatory system.

Q. 568. In members of the phylum Ectoprocta developmental stages of marine species include

(*a*) a cyphonautes larva
(*b*) a cydippid larva
(*c*) an actinotroch larva
(*d*) a dipleurula larva

Q. 569. A statoblast is

(*a*) an excretory mechanism in fresh-water ectoprocts
(*b*) an excretory mechanism in marine ectoprocts
(*c*) an asexual development mechanism in fresh-water ectoprocts
(*d*) an asexual development mechanism in marine ectoprocts.

Q. 570. For convenience of study, the nervous system is often divided into three parts

(*a*) the brain, the cord, the nerves
(*b*) the central, the peripheral and autonomic systems
(*c*) the brain, the peripheral system and the parasympathetic system
(*d*) the central, the sympathetic and the parasympathetic systems.

Q. 571. Chemical agents which transfer the nerve impulse across a synapse are called neurohumors or transmitter substances. Two substances which function as neurohumors are

(*a*) sympathin and ATP
(*b*) DNA and RNA
(*c*) sympathin and acetylcholine
(*d*) acetylcholine and acetyl CoA.

Q. 572. Newborn guinea pigs can walk while newborn rats cannot. This is because

(*a*) guinea pigs are smarter than rats
(*b*) the nerve circuits of the rat are more elaborate than those of the guinea pig
(*c*) maturation in the neurophysiological sense occurs before birth in guinea pigs and after birth in rats
(*d*) rats don't have the necessary enzymes at birth.

Q. 573. Which statement about the sponges is not true?

(*a*) There is no nervous tissue in the sponge and there is little coordination of activities
(*b*) Sponges reproduce asexually by budding and sexually by means of eggs and sperm
(*c*) After being squeezed through bolting cloth, the individual sponge cells collect and reorganize into a new sponge
(*d*) The capacity for regeneration is very low among the sponges.

Q. 574. The Porifera are distinguished from all other animals by the fact that

(*a*) they are unicellular
(*b*) the principal opening is an exit opening
(*c*) the single opening serves for both intake of food and discharge of waste
(*d*) reproduction is both sexual and asexual.

Q. 575. Our prehuman ancestors abandoned arboreal life probably because

(*a*) they became more intelligent, hence more curious
(*b*) they could not compete with arboreal birds, monkeys, and insects
(*c*) trees became less abundant
(*d*) trees were still too small to support their increasing size.

Q. 576. At the beginning of the Paleozoic

(*a*) all major phyla were already established
(*b*) all major plant phyla were already established
(*c*) all major animal phyla were already established
(*d*) most phyla were not yet established.

Q. 577. **Pouched mammals are found largely in**

(*a*) Madagascar
(*b*) China
(*c*) Africa
(*d*) Australia.

Q. 578. **The line leading to man branched off from that leading to apes about**

(*a*) 1 million years ago
(*b*) 30 million years ago
(*c*) 50 million years ago
(*d*) 75 million years ago.

Q. 579. **The earliest man (in the tool-making sense) now known was**

(*a*) *Oreopithecus*
(*b*) *Australopithecus*
(*c*) *Zinjanthropus*
(*d*) *Pithecanthropus.*

Q. 580. **Still in existence today are representatives of**

(*a*) ostracods
(*b*) placoderm
(*c*) ostracoderms
(*d*) ammonites.

Q. 581. **The earliest fossil reptiles are the**

(*a*) dinosaurs
(*b*) cotylosaurs
(*c*) plesiosaurs
(*d*) labrinthodonts.

Q. 582. **Among primates, color vision probably evolved first in**

(*a*) tarsiers
(*b*) monkeys
(*c*) apes
(*d*) lemurs.

Q. 583. **The hominid foot is most like that of**

(*a*) chimphanzees

(*b*) gibbons
(*c*) gorillas
(*d*) orang-utangs.

Q. 584. **In the study of precipitin tests as biochemical evidences for evolution, when one of the following is not verified**

(*a*) the ape is very close to man
(*b*) the lemur is not as close as the apes
(*c*) whales are close to even-toed ungulates
(*d*) the rabbit is close to rodents.

Q. 585. **It appears that man's closest living relatives are the**

(*a*) New World monkeys
(*b*) Old World monkeys
(*c*) lorises
(*d*) anthropoid apes.

Q. 586. **The primates thought to be in the most direct line of human ancestry are the**

(*a*) gorillas
(*b*) orang-utans
(*c*) gibbons
(*d*) australopithecines.

Q. 587. **The first land plants, as indicated by the fossil record, appeared in the**

(*a*) Cambrian
(*b*) Silurian
(*c*) Jurassic
(*d*) Cretaceous.

Q. 588. **Fresh-water ectoprocts differ from marine forms in that they**

(*a*) do not develop statoblasts
(*b*) do develop statoblasts
(*c*) lack a firm exoskeleton
(*d*) have a circular lophophore.

Q. 589. **In members of the phylum Brachiopoda, developmental stages include**

(*a*) a cyphonautes larva
(*b*) a cydippid larva
(*c*) an actinotroch larva
(*d*) none of the above larval stages.

Q. 590. In brachiopods

(*a*) there is an open circulatory system
(*b*) there is a closed circulatory system
(*c*) there is no circulatory system
(*d*) none of the above.

Q. 591. Brachiopods

(*a*) are mostly hermaphroditic
(*b*) are mostly separately sexed
(*c*) have no excretory system
(*d*) have two valves, right and left in position.

Q. 592. If a sponge is sequeezed through bolting cloth

(*a*) each cell becomes a new sponge
(*b*) all cells die
(*c*) about half of the cells individually give rise to new sponges
(*d*) the cells organize into aggregates and develop into new sponges.

Q. 593. The commercially valuable portion of the sponge is:

(*a*) spongin
(*b*) the spicules
(*c*) the entire sponge
(*d*) ascon.

Q. 594. The sponges are

(*a*) multicellular, but do not have true tissues
(*b*) multicellular and have true tissues
(*c*) true metazoans
(*d*) exclusively marine in habitat.

Q. 595. A population is a localized aggregation of

(*a*) individuals of the same species
(*b*) individuals of different species

(*c*) several communities
(*d*) several species.

Q. 596. In bees, males

(*a*) are killed every summer by workers
(*b*) develop from unfertilized eggs
(*c*) do not contribute to the reproduction of the society
(*d*) direct the activities of the workers within the nest.

Q. 597. Speciation is brought about by

(*a*) reproductive barriers
(*b*) polymorphism
(*c*) interbreeding among populations
(*d*) interbreeding within populations

Q. 598. Learning capacity in bees is

(*a*) absent
(*b*) highly limited
(*c*) almost as extensive as in mammals
(*d*) determined by the amount of food given to the larvae.

Q. 599. Species expansion in one direction only is generally typical when an expansion occurs via

(*a*) sweepstake bridges
(*b*) fitter bridges
(*c*) coridor bridges
(*d*) the intermittent bridge over the Bering Straits.

Q. 600. Occupation of the same ecological niche by two or more species generally leads to

(*a*) intraspecific cooperation
(*b*) interspecific cooperation
(*c*) intraspecific competition
(*d*) interspecific competition.

Section VII

Q. 601. When the citric acid cycle is stopped by an inhibitor

(*a*) cell respiration stops
(*b*) cell respiration continues
(*c*) no change is noted
(*d*) phosphate is used up.

Q. 602. Thiamine is required in respiration for

(*a*) the removal of CO_2 from pyruvic acid
(*b*) the synthesis of a hydrogen carrier
(*c*) the removal of hydrogen from acetic acid
(*d*) the formation of lipoic acid.

Q. 603. In respiration, pyruvic acid is

(*a*) one of the steps in the citric acid cycle
(*b*) formed only if oxygen is not available
(*c*) broken down into a 2-carbon fragment and CO_2
(*d*) the result of fatty acid breakdown.

Q. 604. Transmination of glutamic acid yields

(*a*) otaloacebic acid
(*b*) α-ketoglutaric acid
(*c*) succinic acid
(*d*) pyruvic acid.

Q. 605. If the amount of food eaten daily by a healthy college student produced 1000 Calories, he would probably

(*a*) retain his original weight
(*b*) gain weight
(*c*) lose weight
(*d*) gain or lose weight, depending on his original weight.

Q. 606. The greatest amount of energy is obtained from a gram of

(*a*) fat
(*b*) carbohydrate
(*c*) protein
(*d*) mixed fats, carbohydrates and protein.

Q. 607. A lumberjack at work exhibits

(*a*) greater basal metabolic rate than a student when studying
(*b*) a lesser basal metabolic rate than a lumberjack asleep
(*c*) no basal metabolic rate
(*d*) None of these.

Q. 608. A Calorie is the amount of energy required to

(*a*) change one liter of water to one kilogram of ice
(*b*) change one liter of water to steam
(*c*) raise a liter of water through one degree Centigrade
(*d*) oxidize one liter of water completely.

Q. 609. A species of Sarcodina parasitic in man is:

(*a*) *Balanitidium coli*
(*b*) *Euglena viridis*
(*c*) *Plasmodium vivax*
(*d*) *Entamoeba histolytica.*

Q. 610. The stage of the malarial parasite which is infective to man is

(*a*) gametocyte
(*b*) trophozoite
(*c*) oocyst
(*d*) sporozoite.

Q. 611. Digestion in most free-living protozoa is carried on within

(*a*) plastids
(*b*) vacuoles
(*c*) the gullet
(*d*) the mouth

Q. 612. Water regulation is carried on in amoeba by means of

(*a*) pseudopodia
(*b*) plasmasol
(*c*) plasmagel
(*d*) contractile vacuoles

Q. 613. Tapirs are

(*a*) endemic today

(*b*) cosmopolitan today
(*c*) now gradually becoming cosmopolitan
(*d*) on the verge of total extinction.

Q. 614. A syngen is

(*a*) equivalent to a taxonomic species
(*b*) a mating type
(*c*) a reproductive unit encompassing parts of two or more species.
(*d*) a reproductive unit within a taxonomic species.

Q. 615. The limits of an ecological niche are determined mainly by

(*a*) biological factors
(*b*) physical factors
(*c*) both biological and physical factors
(*d*) the developmental stage a population has attained in its life cycle.

Q. 616. In the evolution of the arthropods biramous appendages were modified to form many structures but not to form

(*a*) walking legs
(*b*) wings
(*c*) mandibles
(*d*) maxillae.

Q. 617. The appearance of gill slits in the early embryonic development of all vertebrates would indicate that

(*a*) developing mammalian embryos, surrounded by embryonic fluids, apparently use gills in external respiration
(*b*) fish, amphibia, reptiles, birds and mammals are probably descendants from a common ancestor
(*c*) vestigial structures have a function in early embryonic development
(*d*) phylogeny recapitulates ontogeny.

Q. 618. Members of the class nematomorpha

(*a*) are superficially segmented
(*b*) have no functional digestive system in the adult
(*c*) have a protonephridial excretory system
(*d*) are all hermaphroditic.

Q. 619. Members of the phylum Entoprocta

(*a*) are largely restricted to fresh water
(*b*) have both mouth and anus opening within the anterior circlet of tentacles
(*c*) have the mouth but not the anus opening within the anterior circlet of tentacles
(*d*) have no excretory systems.

Q. 620. Endodermal cells in members of the phylum Mesozoa are

(*a*) reproductive
(*b*) digestive
(*c*) absent
(*d*) excretory.

Q. 621. The basic structure of members of the phylum Mesozoa is

(*a*) triploblastic
(*b*) diploblastic with ectoderm and endoderm
(*c*) two-layered, but the inner layer is entirely reproductive
(*d*) unicellular.

Q. 622. In some invertebrates the process of union between eggs and sperm is best summarized by

(*a*) fusion of the egg and sperm plasma membranes, rupture of the acrosome, presumably liberation of lytic enzymes, egg cytoplasmic cone formation, movement of the sperm nucleus into the cone, cone withdrawal and sperm nuclear incorporation into the egg
(*b*) egg cytoplasmic cone formation to meet the sperm, fusion of egg and sperm plasma membrane, rupture of acrosome, liberation of lytic enzymes permitting some retraction and sperm nuclear incorporation into the egg
(*c*) sperm acrosomal rupture, liberation of lytic enzymes, acrosomal tubule formation, contact and fusion of egg and sperm plasma membranes, bulging and withdrawal, after incorporation of the sperm nucleus, of the egg cytoplasm
(*d*) penetration of the jelly coat by an acrosomal tubule

after acrosome rupture, lytic enzyme activity allowing egg cytoplasmic bulging, migration of sperm nucleus into the egg and withdrawal of the cytoplasmic bulge.

Q. 623. In tapeworms, propagation from host to host is accomplished by

(*a*) active transfer
(*b*) passive transfer
(*c*) both active and passive transfer
(*d*) hyperparasitism.

Q. 624. Viruses are

(*a*) facultative ectoparasites
(*b*) obligatory ectoparasites
(*c*) facultative endoparasites
(*d*) obligatory endoparasites.

Q. 625. Termites and the flagellates in the intestine of these insects form an association called

(*a*) mutualism
(*b*) commensalism
(*c*) parasitism
(*d*) hyperparasitism.

Q. 626. Mimicry is an example of

(*a*) symbiosis
(*b*) polymorphism
(*c*) protective interdependence
(*d*) nutritional interdependence.

Q. 627. In an ecological succession, the biomass tends to

(*a*) remain constant
(*b*) increase
(*c*) decrease
(*d*) vary according to the type of succession.

Q. 628. The nutritional base of an ecosystem is formed by its

(*a*) abiotic components
(*b*) autotrophic components

(*c*) heterotrophic components
(*d*) saprotrophic components.

Q. 629. If man is part of a community, he usually

(*a*) is at the base of a food pyramid
(*b*) is at the top of a food pyramid
(*c*) is at any level of a food pyramid
(*d*) None of these.

Q. 630. In a climax community, the biomass tends to

(*a*) remain constant
(*b*) increase gradually
(*c*) decrease gradually
(*d*) fluctuate impredictably.

Q. 631. In an ecosystem, species diversity and the sizes of organisms present tend to be

(*a*) more or less unrelated
(*b*) related, but in different ways in different cases
(*c*) directly proportional
(*d*) inversely proportional.

Q. 632. In the life cycle of a liver fluke, the larval stage present within a fish is a

(*a*) cercaria
(*b*) redia
(*c*) miracidium
(*d*) sporocyst.

Q. 633. If anti-whale serum is prepared and then used for testing relationships, the greatest precipitation will be found in which of the following tests?

(*a*) rat
(*b*) pig
(*c*) horse
(*d*) man.

Q. 634. A primitive vertebrate forelimb has skeletal parts in the following order

(*a*) radius, ulna, humerus, carpals, metacarpals, phalanges

(*b*) radius, fibula, ulna, carpals, phalanges
(*c*) femur, radius and ulna, metacarpals, carpals, phalanges.
(*d*) humerus, radius and ulna, carpals, metacarpals, phalanges.

Q. 635. In the evolution of arthropods the primitive biramous appendages have given rise to

(*a*) uniramous legs
(*b*) mouthparts
(*c*) wings
(*d*) only A and B above.

Q. 636. Ammonia, which is converted to urea, comes from

(*a*) "building blocks" of proteins
(*b*) deaminization of cellulose
(*c*) hydrolysis of pentose sugars
(*d*) metabolism of fat.

Q. 637. The constancy of the internal environment is called

(*a*) homeotypy
(*b*) coelothermy
(*c*) anastasis
(*d*) homeostasis.

Q. 638. The adult kidney characteristic of fish and amphibia is

(*a*) holonephros
(*b*) pronephros
(*c*) opisthonephros
(*d*) metanephros.

Q. 639. An organelle is

(*a*) a localized cellular differentiation
(*b*) a covering on an unicellular organism
(*c*) a cellular differentiation involved with locomotion
(*d*) a degenerate, nonfunctional organ.

Q. 640. A distinguishing characteristic of the class Ciliata is

(*a*) pseudopodia
(*b*) micronucleus and macronucleus

(*c*) cysts
(*d*) spores.

Q. 641. The cilia of *Paramecium*

(*a*) have the basic 9 + 2 arrangement of fibrils and hydrolyze ATP to ADP
(*b*) do not carry on metabolism
(*c*) beat independently of neighboring cilia
(*d*) are very small in number compared to the other ciliates.

Q. 642. Reproduction in paramecia occurs by

(*a*) sexual means only
(*b*) asexual means only
(*c*) releasing DNA into the medium which is taken up by another animal
(*d*) sexual and asexual means.

Q. 643. The Mastigophora have which of the following organs of locomotion?

(*a*) cilia
(*b*) pseudopodia
(*c*) flagella
(*d*) fins.

Q. 644. The littoral zone is populated by

(*a*) plankton
(*b*) nekton
(*c*) benthos
(*d*) plankton, nekton, and benthos.

Q. 645. The taiga is characterized by

(*a*) forests composed of single species of trees
(*b*) forests composed of many species of trees
(*c*) absence of trees
(*d*) absence of forests.

Q. 646. At sea depths below 1,000 feet

(*a*) plants are absent
(*b*) animals are absent

(*c*) both plants and animals are absent
(*d*) both plants and animals are present.

Q. 647. The water over the abyssal plain represents the

(*a*) littoral zone
(*b*) neritic zone
(*c*) oceanic zone
(*d*) photic zone.

Q. 648. Both deserts and tundras are characterized by

(*a*) little-precipitation
(*b*) low average annual temperatures
(*c*) short growing seasons
(*d*) absence of warm-blooded animals.

Q. 649. All oceans have virtually the same

(*a*) buoyancy
(*b*) density
(*c*) proportions of salts
(*d*) salinity.

Q. 650. The movement of ocean water between equator and North Pole is such that

(*a*) warm water flows north along the sea floor
(*b*) cold water flows north along the sea floor
(*c*) warm water flows south along the sea floor
(*d*) cold water flows south along the sea floor.

Q. 651. Scyphozoan medusae mature directly from free-swimming

(*a*) planula larvae
(*b*) scyphistoma larvae
(*c*) actinula larvae
(*d*) ephyra larvae.

Q. 652. Ctenophores

(*a*) are largely separately sexed
(*b*) undergo determinate cleavage
(*c*) are diploblastic
(*d*) develop via a planula larva.

Q. 653. The comb rows of ctenophores are underlaid by the

(*a*) tentacular canals
(*b*) transverse canals
(*c*) aboral canals
(*d*) meridional canals.

Q. 654. Ctenophores include

(*a*) neither polymorphic or colonial types
(*b*) both polymorphic and colonial types
(*c*) polymorphic but not colonial types
(*d*) colonial but not polymorphic types.

Q. 655. Movement in ctenophores results from

(*a*) jet propulsion
(*b*) muscular activity
(*c*) swimming tentacles
(*d*) coordinated ciliary activity.

Q. 656. The conversion of ammonia to atmospheric nitrogen is accomplished by

(*a*) nitrogen-fixing bacteria
(*b*) nitrifying bacteria
(*c*) denitrifying bacteria
(*d*) decay-causing bacteria.

Q. 657. Chemosynthetic organisms

(*a*) are dependent upon sunlight as a source of energy
(*b*) use energy derived from simple organic chemicals to synthesize carbohydrates
(*c*) use energy derived from certain inorganic compounds to synthesize carbohydrates
(*d*) convert atmospheric nitrogen into carbohydrates.

Q. 658. Sulfur bacteria are able to

(*a*) cat elemental sulfur
(*b*) live as parasites
(*c*) obtain energy by breaking down inorganic compounds
(*d*) use heat for energy.

Q. 659. Water is not required directly for the completion of the

(*a*) oxygen cycle
(*b*) carbon cycle
(*c*) nitrogen cycle
(*d*) hydrogen cycle.

Q. 660. Tropical seas tend to have

(*a*) the greatest abundance of marine life
(*b*) the highest salinities
(*c*) relatively little species diversity
(*d*) no thermoclines the year round.

Q. 661. During the day, plankton tends to be concentrated

(*a*) in sunlit surface waters
(*b*) in dim layers below the surface
(*c*) below the thermocline,
(*d*) randomly throughout the waters above the thermocline.

Q. 662. The results of many experiments showed that strains of *Neurospora* derived from mutagenic treatment

(*a*) were the same as the original strain
(*b*) required a specific compound in the medium
(*c*) were all morphologically distinguishable from the original strain
(*d*) had lost the ability to carry out DNA replication.

Q. 663. The amino acid substitutions that cause abnormal hemoglobins

(*a*) are all in the α-chain
(*b*) are all in the β-chain
(*c*) are all in the heme group
(*d*) are very specific and occur in both chains.

Q. 664. The method whereby the hookworm enters its host is through

(*a*) the mouth
(*b*) cuts and wounds
(*c*) active larval penetration of the skin
(*d*) introduction into the blood by mosquitoes.

Q. 665. *Trichinella spirilis* is passed from one host to man

(*a*) by eating of infected, uncooked pork
(*b*) through the feet
(*c*) by a mosquito
(*d*) by eating poorly washed fresh vegetables.

Q. 666. A triplet genetic code can theoretically specify

(*a*) 3 amino acids
(*b*) 9 amino acids
(*c*) 27 amino acids
(*d*) 64 amino acids.

Q. 667. In the development of an organism, enzymes serving specific functions change; this change

(*a*) has not been shown to have a genetic basis
(*b*) has been shown to have a genetic basis
(*c*) is always due to the addition of a metal ion
(*d*) is so rapid that one form of the enzyme is immediately substituted by the new form.

Q. 668. The transfilter technique of studying potential tissue interactions

(*a*) clearly eliminates a chemical action of one tissue on another
(*b*) shows that each tissue has a very precise interrelationship with another tissue in its development
(*c*) shows that all tissues are influenced by relatively nonspecific stimuli from other tissues.
(*d*) shows that some tissues have very specific relationships to other tissues while others are less specific.

Q. 669. Digestion in hydra occurs

(*a*) extracellularly only
(*b*) intracellularly only
(*c*) extracellularly and intracellularly
(*d*) in swellings on the epidermis

Q. 670. A colony of *Obelia* consists of

(*a*) nutritive zooids or reproductive zooids, the hydrocaulus and the hydrorhiza

(*b*) nutritive zooids, the hydrocaulus and the hydrorhiza
(*c*) reproductive zooids, the hydrocaulus and the hydrorhiza
(*d*) nutritive and reproductive zooids, the hydrocaulus and hydrorhiza.

Q. 671. Metagenesis is

(*a*) the phenomenon of alternation of generations
(*b*) development without fertilization
(*c*) formation of a syncytium
(*d*) also called strobilization.

Q. 672. The medusae of *Obelia*

(*a*) are true jellyfishes
(*b*) possess a velum
(*c*) do not possess a velum
(*d*) are vegetative stages.

Q. 673. Porifera form a

(*a*) metazoan grade
(*b*) eumetazoan branch
(*c*) parazoan phylum
(*d*) mesozoan subgrade.

Q. 674. Sponge gametes usually arise from

(*a*) archeocytes
(*b*) pinacocytes
(*c*) choanocytes
(*d*) porocytes.

Q. 675. The mesogloea contains various kinds of

(*a*) pinacocytes
(*b*) choanocytes
(*c*) amoebocytes
(*d*) myocytes.

Q. 676. Myocytes of sponges may occur in

(*a*) the external epithelium
(*b*) the mesogloea
(*c*) the choanocyte epithelium
(*d*) any of the above body parts.

Q. 677. Water leaves the body of a sponge via

(*a*) ostia
(*b*) oscula
(*c*) apopyles
(*d*) porocytes.

Q. 678. In a syconoid sponge, water enters the body via

(*a*) ostia
(*b*) oscula
(*c*) apopyles
(*d*) porocytes.

Q. 679. During the time when the most extensive coal deposits were formed, there were in existence

(*a*) very few kinds of animals
(*b*) no chordates
(*c*) mainly protozoans and sponges
(*d*) all the major phyla of animals.

Q. 680. Which of the following lists of geological eras is in correct order?

(*a*) Cenozoic, Mesozoic, Paleozoic, Proterozoic, Archaeozoic
(*b*) Mesozoic, Paleozoic, Proterozoic, Cenozoic, Archeozoic
(*c*) Mesozoic, Proterozoic, Paleozoic, Archaeozoic
(*d*) Paleozoic, Mesozoic, Cenozoic, Archaeozoic, Proterozoic.

Q. 681. According to Mayr all human fossils should be placed in the genus *Homo*. Using this system the Java man would be called

(*a*) *Homo sapiens*
(*b*) *Homo transvaalensis*
(*c*) *Homo erectus*
(*d*) *Homo coloensis*.

Q. 682. Fossils are most commonly found in

(*a*) igneous rocks

(*b*) sedimentary rocks
(*c*) metamorphic rocks
(*d*) graphite.

Q. 683. The vasoconstrictor produced by the kidneys is

(*a*) vasopressin
(*b*) uremia
(*c*) renin
(*d*) nephrostrictin.

Q. 684. The correct order of amino acids in the mammalian urea producing cycle is

(*a*) urea –> ornithine –> arginine –> citrulline
(*b*) ornithine –> alanine –> urinine
(*c*) ornithine –> citrulline –> arginine
(*d*) ornithine –> urinine –> arginine.

Q. 685. The pronephric kidney type is the functional type in the following adult organisms:

(*a*) frog
(*b*) man
(*c*) goldfish
(*d*) none of the above.

Q. 686. The following kinds of organisms have the metanephric kidney

(*a*) mammal
(*b*) amphibian
(*c*) reptile
(*d*) A and C above.

Q. 687. In an asconoid sponge, water enters the body via

(*a*) ostia
(*b*) oscula
(*c*) apopyles
(*d*) porocytes.

Q. 688. Demispongiae are very largely of

(*a*) asconoid type
(*b*) syconoid type

(*c*) leuconoid type
(*d*) asconoid or syconoid type.

Q. 689. A syncytial construction is characteristic of

(*a*) calcareous sponges
(*b*) glass sponges
(*c*) horny sponges
(*d*) many sponges of all classes.

Q. 690. A definite external epithelium is lacking in

(*a*) calcareous sponges
(*b*) glass sponges
(*c*) horny sponges
(*d*) many sponges of all classes.

Q. 691. The narrowest openings among the following are provided by

(*a*) ostia
(*b*) oscula
(*c*) prosopyles
(*d*) apopyles.

Q. 692. Most sponges are

(*a*) separately sexed
(*b*) cross-fertilizing hermaphrodites
(*c*) self-fertilizing hermaphrodites
(*d*) isogamous.

Q. 693. An amphiblastula forms during the development of

(*a*) *Farrea*
(*b*) *Halisarca*
(*c*) *Hycon*
(*d*) *Leucosolenia.*

Q. 694. The spicules characteristic particularly of glass sponges are

(*a*) tetractinic
(*b*) hexactinic
(*c*) triactinic
(*d*) monactinic.

Q. 695. Spongioblasts are found in

(*a*) calcareous sponges
(*b*) glass sponges
(*c*) horny sponges
(*d*) all skeleton-forming sponges.

Q. 696. Large food particles in sponges are trapped by

(*a*) choanocytes
(*b*) porocytes
(*c*) pinacocytes
(*d*) archeocytes.

Q. 697. Mesoder cells in Mesozoa are conspicuously

(*a*) digestive
(*b*) reproductive
(*c*) gamete-forming
(*d*) absent.

Q. 698. Gemmules are formed characteristically by

(*a*) most marine sponges
(*b*) most freshwater sponges
(*c*) some marine and freshwater sponges in each class
(*d*) most marine and freshwater sponges in each class.

Q. 699. It is most likely that Parazoa have evolved

(*a*) from protozoa
(*b*) into Mesozoa
(*c*) from yet unknown stocks of algae
(*d*) into no other animal type.

Q. 700. Sponge development is

(*a*) regulative in some known cases
(*b*) mosaic in some known cases
(*c*) regulative in all known cases
(*d*) mosaic in all known cases.

Section VIII

Q. 701. The liver fluke belongs to the phylum Platyhelminthes and class

(*a*) Turbellaria
(*b*) Scyphozoa
(*c*) Cestoda
(*d*) Trematoda.

Q. 702. Free-living Platyhelminthes are similar to the Coelenterata in which one of the following respects?

(*a*) Platyhelminthes have but one opening into the digestive cavity
(*b*) Platyhelminthes are bilaterally symmetrical
(*c*) Platyhelminthes have a well-developed mesoderm
(*d*) Platyhelminthes have a definite and permanent front end.

Q. 703. Four of the following are characteristics of the common flatworm, *Planaria*. Which one is *not* characteristic of this animal?

(*a*) a segmented body
(*b*) a much branched and lobed gastro-vascular cavity
(*c*) a ciliated body
(*d*) flame cells in the excretory system.

Q. 704. The primitive condition in the coelenterates is probably

(*a*) the medusa
(*b*) the planula form
(*c*) the trochophore form
(*d*) alternation of generations.

Q. 705. Polymorphism probably reaches its greatest diversification

(*a*) in the coelenterates
(*b*) in the protozoa
(*c*) in the porifera
(*d*) in the insects.

Q. 706. Which of the following is the correct sequence for the life cycle of *Aurelia*, a true jellyfish?

(*a*) medusa, planula, polyp, scyphistoma, ephyra
(*b*) medusa, ephyra, planula, polyp, scyphistoma
(*c*) medusa, planula, scyphistoma, polyp, ephyra
(*d*) medusa, planula, ephyra, polyp, scyphistoma.

Q. 707. Most coelenterates are

(*a*) separately sexed
(*b*) self-fertilizing monoecious forms
(*c*) cross-fertilizing monoecious forms
(*d*) asexual, reproducing only by budding.

Q. 708. As a group, coelenterates are

(*a*) omnivorous
(*b*) carnivorous
(*c*) herbivorous
(*d*) able to subsist as holotrophs as well as saprotrophs.

Q. 709. Stinging threads with closed ends and adhesive functions are the

(*a*) penetrants
(*b*) cnidocils
(*c*) cnidoblasts
(*d*) volvants.

Q. 710. Scyphozoa are fundamentally

(*a*) tetramerous
(*b*) hexamerous
(*c*) octomerous
(*d*) polymerous.

Q. 711. Epithellomuscular cells occur in

(*a*) primitive coelenterates of all classes
(*b*) Hydrozoa
(*c*) Scyphozoa
(*d*) Anthozoa.

Q. 712. The most primitive form of the coelenterate mesogloea appears to occur in

(*a*) scyphomedusae
(*b*) hydrozoan polyps

(*c*) scyphozoan polyps
(*d*) hydromedusae.

Q. 713. Budding may not generally give rise to

(*a*) new polyps from parental medusae
(*b*) new medusae from parental polyps
(*c*) new polyps from parental polyps
(*d*) new medusae from parental medusae.

Q. 714. Most coelenterates are

(*a*) separately sexed
(*b*) self-fertilizing hermaphrodites
(*c*) cross-fertilizing hermaphrodites
(*d*) asexual reproduction occurring largely through budding.

Q. 715. Cleavage in most coelenterates is

(*a*) bilateral and meroblastic
(*b*) radial and holoblastic
(*c*) bilateral and holoblastic
(*d*) radial and meroblastic.

Q. 716. Human beings who suffer from the sickle-cell trait produce offspring in the following ratio: 1 normal, 2 sickle-cell trait and 1 serverely affected sickle-celled (sickle-cell disease). This is an example of

(*a*) factor interaction
(*b*) lack of dominance
(*c*) multiple factors
(*d*) multiple alleles.

Q. 717. The graded series of eye colors (from red to white) is an example of

(*a*) factor interaction
(*b*) lack of dominance
(*c*) multiple factors
(*d*) multiple alleles.

Q. 718. *Euglena* normally utilizes holophytic nutrition, whereby some food is

(*a*) ingested
(*b*) egested
(*c*) acquired parasitically
(*d*) synthesized by the use of chlorophyll.

Q. 719. In single celled animal such as *Paramecium*, the process by which two animals join and exchange nuclear material is called

(*a*) copulation
(*b*) conjugation
(*c*) cleavage
(*d*) fertilization.

Q. 720. From your study of amoeba, you should have concluded that

(*a*) most amoeba are parasitic
(*b*) all protoplasm is composed of cells
(*c*) animals fall into two types
(*d*) a single cell can carry on all life processes.

Q. 721. Cell respiration can be stopped

(*a*) by carbon monoxide but not cyanide
(*b*) by cyanide but not carbon monoxide
(*c*) by inhibiting any enzyme in the citric acid cycle
(*d*) by inhibiting any enzyme.

Q. 722. In respiration, each molecule of glucose

(*a*) yields four molecules of pyruvic acid
(*b*) loses five hydrogens
(*c*) loses three hydrogens
(*d*) yields two moecules of pyruvic acid.

Q. 723. The process of respiration

(*a*) is literally a fire
(*b*) is quite similar in all organisms
(*c*) usually does not involve oxygen
(*d*) usually does not result in CO_2 production.

Q. 724. FAD appears to function

(*a*) as a vitamin

(b) as an electron carrier
(c) as a hormone
(d) as a hydrolytic enzyme.

Q. 725. The energy released in respiration is trapped by

(a) adenosine diphosphate
(b) adenosine triphosphate
(c) high-energy bonds
(d) adenosine monophosphate.

Q. 726. The breakdown of a 6-carbon sugar molecule in respiration results in

(a) the production of carbon monoxide
(b) two molecules of pyruvic acid
(c) a 2-carbon sugar
(d) loss of ATP.

Q. 727. Most of the energy-yield in respiration results from

(a) fuel breakdown
(b) conversion of glucose to pyruvic acid
(c) hydrogen transfer
(d) conversion of pyruvic acid to acetyl CoA.

Q. 728. Respiration generates far lower temperatures than a fire because

(a) the two are fundamentally different processes
(b) simpler substances are involved in respiration
(c) respiration involves only very small amounts of substance at any given time
(d) energy is liberated in a fire from many chemical bonds simultaneously.

Q. 729. In carbohydrate metabolism in cells, production of carbon dioxide

(a) results from the breakdown of ATP
(b) takes place in the citric acid cycle
(c) occurs each time a molecule of ATP is made
(d) takes place each time a dehydrogenation occurs.

Q. 730. The production of energy by the breakdown of glucose

(*a*) is like burning, only slower
(*b*) involves an expenditure of ATP
(*c*) involves a net loss of ATP
(*d*) involves a net loss of water.

Q. 731. The first step in the utilization of glucose in metabolism consists of the formation of

(*a*) ATP
(*b*) glucose-phosphate
(*c*) pyruvic acid
(*d*) high-energy bonds.

Q. 732. When fatty acids are burned, they are first converted to

(*a*) 6-carbon phosphate
(*b*) pyruvic acid
(*c*) glycerin
(*d*) 2-carbon compounds.

Q. 733. DPN is related chemically to

(*a*) riboflavin
(*b*) adrenalin
(*c*) nicotinic acid
(*d*) thiamine.

Q. 734. Acetyl_CoA enters the citric acid cycle by combining with

(*a*) ketoglutaric acid
(*b*) succinic acid
(*c*) citric acid
(*d*) oxaloacetic acid.

Q. 735. Evidence that growth-controlling gradients exist in planarians is provided by which of the following?

(*a*) The many branched digestive tract extends into every portion of the body
(*b*) A double nerve cord runs the length of the body, with the major ganglia located in the head end
(*c*) If the eyes of a planarian are destroyed, the organism can still respond to light
(*d*) If one of these worms is cut transversely in half, the head end will develop a tail and the tail end will produce a head.

Q. 736. The theory of C.M. Child says that a metabolic gradient exists in *Planaria*. This decreasing gradient runs

(*a*) postero-anterior
(*b*) antero-posterior
(*c*) dorsi-ventral
(*d*) ventro-dorsal.

Q. 737. The muscular system as found in *Planaria* consists of

(*a*) circular and logitudinal muscles
(*b*) circular, longitudinal, and dorso-ventral muscles
(*c*) circular and dorso-ventral muscles
(*d*) longitudinal and dorso-ventral.

Q. 738. Organic compounds are

(*a*) those compounds which contain carbon and usually contain carbon-hydrogen bonds
(*b*) all the compounds of carbon
(*c*) compounds synthesized only in living cells
(*d*) compounds which contain carbon–these being a very small percentage of the total number of known chemical compounds.

Q. 739. The pH of a solution containing 0.00001 moles of hydrogen ions is

(*a*) 4
(*b*) 5
(*c*) 6
(*d*) 7.

Q. 740. A substance which acts to resist a change in pH is called

(*a*) a buffer
(*b*) an electrolyte
(*c*) an anion
(*d*) a salt.

Q. 741. In an animal which has a diploid chromosome number of eight, each gamete will contain how many chromosomes?

(*a*) eight
(*b*) four

(*c*) two
(*d*) six.

Q. 742. The three "major" components of atoms are

(*a*) protons, neutrons, mesons
(*b*) protons, neutrons, electrons
(*c*) protons, electrons, α-particles
(*d*) protons, mesons, electrons

Q. 743. The atomic number of an element is

(*a*) the number of protons in the nucleus
(*b*) the number of nucleons in the nucleus
(*c*) the number of electrons in the outer shell
(*d*) the number of isotopes of an element.

Q. 744. The hydrogen atom consists of

(*a*) one proton and one neutron
(*b*) one proton and one electron
(*c*) one neutron and one electron
(*d*) two protons and one electron.

Q. 745. Orbitals may be divided into two classes

(*a*) atomic and molecular
(*b*) atomic and subatomic
(*c*) subatomic and molecular
(*d*) low-energy and high-energy.

Q. 746. Most of what is known about heredity

(*a*) was discovered before Darwin announced his hypothesis on the origin of species
(*b*) was discovered by Mendel in the nineteenth century
(*c*) has been discovered since the turn of the century
(*d*) was discovered by Spallazani and Kölreuter in the eighteenth century.

Q. 747. The term *genotype* designates which of the following?

(*a*) the appearance of an individual
(*b*) the genetic make-up of an individual
(*c*) the appearance of a race
(*d*) the genetic make-up of a race.

Q. 748. The classical mendelian ratios for a monohybrid and dihybrid cross, respectively, are:

(*a*) 3:1 and 9:3:3:1
(*b*) 1:2:1 and 9:3:3:1
(*c*) 3:1 and 9:6:1
(*d*) 3:1 and 9:7.

Q. 749. Establishment of an attraction between eggs and sperm, at least in some invertebrates, appears to be assisted by

(*a*) substances primarily located in the egg coat
(*b*) substances located in the plasma membrane of the egg
(*c*) substances located in the plasma membrane of the sperm
(*d*) substances located in the acrosome of the sperm.

Q. 750. The correct comparison between a period of development in sea urchin and in frog is

(*a*) vegetal pole invagination in sea urchin, subequatorial invagination in frog
(*b*) mesodermal pouch formation in sea urchin, multiple mesodermal invagination from epiblast in frog
(*c*) spiral cleavage in sea urchin, holoblastic cleavage in frog
(*d*) archenteron formation in sea urchin, no archenteron formation in frog.

Q. 751. The smallest number of cells among several blastomeres which can give rise to the mesoderm of an organism is known to be

(*a*) 1
(*b*) 4
(*c*) 16
(*d*) 64.

Q. 752. In normal development, the process of neurulation in amphibian and bird

(*a*) is one of self-differentiation
(*b*) is one of tissue interaction between ectoderm and mesoderm

(*c*) is one of tissue interaction between mesoderm and endoderm
(*d*) is one of tissue interaction between ectoderm and endoderm.

Q. 753. The names of the nucleic acids ribonucleic and deoxyribonucleic are

(*a*) related to the purines present in each
(*b*) related to the pyrimidines present in each
(*c*) related to the sugars present in each
(*d*) related to the base composition of each.

Q. 754. Usually, the ribonucleic acids are divided into three subgroups:

(*a*) ribosomal, messenger and transfer
(*b*) ribosomal, nuclear and transfer
(*c*) cytoplasmic, nuclear and ribosomal
(*d*) cytoplasmic, nuclear and messenger.

Q. 755. Flatworm cleavage is

(*a*) regulative and bilateral
(*b*) mosaic and spiral
(*c*) regulative and spiral
(*d*) mosaic and bilateral.

Q. 756. Mueller's larva is characteristic of

(*a*) acoels
(*b*) rhabdocoels
(*c*) triclads
(*d*) polyclads.

Q. 757. A miracidium larva of flukes is

(*a*) untailed but ciliated
(*b*) tailed but unciliated
(*c*) tailed and ciliated
(*d*) untailed and unciliated.

Q. 758. Ectolecithal eggs are not characteristic of

(*a*) rhabdocoels
(*b*) alloeocoels

(*c*) triclads
(*d*) polyclads.

Q. 759. A straight intestine with lateral diverticula is characteristic of

(*a*) acoels
(*b*) rhabdocoels
(*c*) alloeocoels
(*d*) triclads.

Q. 760. The most common mating pattern in tapeworms includes

(*a*) hypodermic impregnation between two worms
(*b*) self-fertilization within the same proglottid
(*c*) cross-fertilization between two proglottids of the same worm
(*d*) cross-fertilization between two different worms.

Q. 761. Redia larvae develop in

(*a*) both *Clonorchis* and *Schistosoma*
(*b*) neither *Clonorchis* nor *Schistosoma*
(*c*) *Clonorchis* but not *Schistosoma*
(*d*) *Schistosoma* but not *Clonorchis*.

Q. 762. Each tapeworm proglottid contains a portion of the

(*a*) acoelomic body cavity
(*b*) saclike digestive system
(*c*) subepidermal nerve net
(*d*) excretory channel system.

Q. 763. Though hermaphroditism is common in flatworms generally, the sexes are separate in

(*a*) *Dugesia*
(*b*) *Schistosoma*
(*c*) *Taenia*
(*d*) *Bdelloura*.

Q. 764. Acoels are without

(*a*) mouth
(*b*) intestine
(*c*) nerve cords
(*d*) mesodermal derivatives.

Q. 765. The copulatory organ of a planarian projects

(*a*) into a sperm sac,
(*b*) into a genital chamber
(*c*) into a copulatory sac
(*d*) into a female worm during mating.

Q. 766. Regeneration in turbellarians may occur readily in

(*a*) both embryos and adults
(*b*) embryos but not adults
(*c*) adults but not embryos
(*d*) neither embryos nor adults.

Q. 767. Polyelads probably have evolved directly from ancestral

(*a*) triclads
(*b*) rhabdocoels
(*c*) alloeocoels
(*d*) acoels.

Q. 768. Fresh-water as well as terrestrial representatives are encountered among

(*a*) acoels
(*b*) triclads
(*c*) free-living trematodes
(*d*) polyclads.

Q. 769. The epidermis of nemertines

(*a*) contains rhabdites
(*b*) is chitin-covered
(*c*) is scleroprotein-covered
(*d*) lies adjacent to the body-wall muscles.

Q. 770. Mueller's and pilidium larvae are alike in their

(*a*) drastic metamorphosis
(*b*) possession of eight epidermal lobes
(*c*) saclike alimentary system
(*d*) conical helmet shape.

Q. 771. Evolutionary affinities appear to be closest between nemertines and

(*a*) trematodes

(*b*) acoels
(*c*) alloeocoels
(*d*) rhabdocoels.

Q. 772. The excretory system in nemertines

(*a*) is absent
(*b*) contains protonephridial flame bulbs
(*c*) includes paired renal glands lying close to the blood vessels
(*d*) exits via the rhynchocoel in some genera.

Q. 773. The circulatory system of nemertines

(*a*) contains blood without cells
(*b*) includes respiratory blood pigments dissolved in plasma
(*c*) includes a dorsal vessel which functions as a heart
(*d*) is closed.

Q. 774. Of the four major classes of organic compounds in living systems, which three are significant sources of energy for organisms?

(*a*) carbohydrates, nucleic acids, proteins
(*b*) carbohydrates, nucleic acids, lipids
(*c*) carbohydrates, lipids, proteins
(*d*) nucleic acids, proteins, lipids.

Q. 775. The compound that functions repeatedly in nature by linking endergonic reactions to exergonic reaction is

(*a*) adenosine
(*b*) adenosine monophosphate
(*c*) adenosine diphosphate
(*d*) adenosine triphosphate.

Q. 776. A cytologist might investigate

(*a*) cells and cell organelles
(*b*) the nature of tissues
(*c*) organs and organ systems
(*d*) parasitic worms.

Q. 777. The branch of zoology that deals with the study of fishes is

(*a*) protozoology
(*b*) ichthyology
(*c*) ecology
(*d*) entomology.

Q. 778. After making careful observations a scientist will collect and analyze his data. The results may prompt him to formalize a general statement known as a(an)

(*a*) idea
(*b*) hypothesis
(*c*) theory
(*d*) law.

Q. 779. The characteristic of living cells to synthesize new cellular materials from simple materials, to oxidize food materials, and to break down living material is referred to as

(*a*) anabolism
(*b*) osmosis
(*c*) catabolism
(*d*) metabolism.

Q. 780. Male rotifers

(*a*) occur at all seasons
(*b*) are larger than females
(*c*) develop from small, unfertilized eggs,
(*d*) usually last over the winter.

Q. 781. Mietic rotifer eggs

(*a*) are diploid and develop into males after being fertilized
(*b*) are haploid and develop into males parthenogenetically
(*c*) are diploid and develop into males parthenogenetically
(*d*) are haploid and develop into males after being fertilized.

Q. 782. The number of different kinds of gametes which are formed by an individual having *n* number of heterozygous allelic pairs located on different chromosomes is

(*a*) 2^n
(*b*) n^2
(*c*) 2_n
(*d*) e^{-n}.

Q. 783. Gene segregation occurs in meiosis in

(*a*) anaphase of the second division
(*b*) metaphase of the second division
(*c*) interphase between the two divisions
(*d*) prophase of the first division.

Q. 784. There are many subdivisions of biology. One of the newer subdivisions is

(*a*) embryology
(*b*) plant biology
(*c*) physiology
(*d*) molecular biology.

Q. 785. There is a hierarchy of organization in biological studies. Which of the following is in proper order?

(*a*) molecules, cells, tissues, organs, organ system, organisms, communities, populations
(*b*) molecules, cells, tissues, organs, organ systems, organisms, populations, communities
(*c*) molecules, tissues, cells, organs, organ systems, organisms, populations, communities
(*d*) cells, molecules, organs, tissues, organ systems, organisms, communities, populations.

Q. 786. The killer property of certain strains of *Paramecium*

(*a*) is due to the presence of kappa particles in the cytoplasm of the organisms
(*b*) allows mating with other killer strains only
(*c*) prevents mating, the killers reproduce only by fission
(*d*) allows strains to show positive geotropism.

Q. 787. A trypanosome

(*a*) is the cause of African Sleeping sickness and is transmitted by the *Anopheles* mosquito
(*b*) is the cause of malaria and is transmitted by the *Anopheles* mosquito
(*c*) is the cause of African sleeping sickness and is transmitted by the tse-tse fly
(*d*) causes malaria and is transmitted by the tse-tse fly.

Q. 788. The malarial parasite is transmitted by

(*a*) the male *Anopheles* mosquito
(*b*) the female *Anopheles* mosquito
(*c*) the tse-tse fly
(*d*) both sexes of the *Anopheles* mosquito.

Q. 789. The most primitive of the Protozoa are

(*a*) the sporozoans
(*b*) the ciliates
(*c*) the flagellates
(*d*) the suctorians.

Q. 790. The probable origin of the Protozoa is form the

(*a*) blue-green algae
(*b*) bacteria
(*c*) viruses
(*d*) green flagellates.

Q. 791. Solenocytic protonephridia occur in

(*a*) rotifers
(*b*) namatodes
(*c*) kinorhynchs
(*d*) priapulids.

Q. 792. The excretory system of nematodes includes

(*a*) solenocytes
(*b*) flame bulbs
(*c*) ventral glands
(*d*) lacunar channels in the epidermis.

Q. 793. Larval molting occurs in

(*a*) rotifers
(*b*) gastortrichs
(*c*) kinorhynchs
(*d*) priapulids.

Q. 794. In Acanthocephala

(*a*) a mouth is present but an intestine is not
(*b*) the lacunar system may serve in food transport

(*c*) the lemnisci achieve proboseis retraction
(*d*) the ligament sacs enclose the excretory organs.

Q. 795. In entoprocts

(*a*) an excretory system is absent
(*b*) the tentacles are solid and ciliated
(*c*) the epidermis is syncytial
(*d*) fertilization occurs internally.

Q. 796. In rotifers

(*a*) an ocellus (if present) is situated at the tip of the dorsal antenna
(*b*) nonparthenogenetic genera are hermaphroditic
(*c*) the corona consists of cilia
(*d*) regeneration potentials are limited in the embryos but are extensive in the adults.

Q. 797. The longest-lived rotifers are those produced from

(*a*) early eggs of young mothers
(*b*) early eggs of old mothers
(*c*) late eggs of young mothers
(*d*) late eggs of old mothers.

Q. 798. In gastrotrichs

(*a*) cellular membranes partition the pseudocoel
(*b*) the musculature is not syncytial
(*c*) the circulatory system is open
(*d*) the animals are fundamentally hermaphroditic.

Q. 799. In kinorhynchs

(*a*) epidermal chords are not present
(*b*) the pharynx is similar to that of gastrotrichs
(*c*) the segmental body design affects the musculature but not the nervous system
(*d*) young larvae already resemble the adults greatly.

Q. 800. In priapulids

(*a*) clusters of flame bulbs open into urogenital ducts
(*b*) the intestine is highly coiled
(*c*) the proboscis is nonretractible
(*d*) the sexes are separate.

Section IX

Q. 801. In nematodes

(*a*) all body-wall muscles are aligned circularly,
(*b*) sprems are amoeboid
(*c*) a chitinous cuticle covers the body
(*d*) males are larger than females in separately sexed species.

Q. 802. Parasitic nematodes living in the intestines of mammals include

(*a*) *Ascaris*
(*b*) *Trichinella*
(*c*) *Necator*
(*d*) *Dracunculus*.

Q. 803. In nematomorphs

(*a*) excretory systems are lacking
(*b*) epidermal chords are conspicuous
(*c*) gastrulation is epibolic
(*d*) a retractible proboscis for attachment develops at the time of metamorphosis.

Q. 804. Most of the adult mesoderm of rotifers arises from

(*a*) ectoderm
(*b*) endoderm
(*c*) both ectoderm and endoderm
(*d*) 4d teloblast cells.

Q. 805. In an entoproct bud, the epidermis arises from

(*a*) ectoderm
(*b*) mesoderm
(*c*) endoderm
(*d*) any of the parental tissues that happen to be on the surface, regardless of their original germ-layer derivation.

Q. 806. After the nematodes, the most common aschelminths are the

(*a*) priapulids
(*b*) gastrotrichs
(*c*) rotifers
(*d*) kinorhynchs.

Q. 807. Moniliformis is a

(*a*) nematode
(*b*) spiny-headed worm
(*c*) hairworm
(*d*) rotifer.

Q. 808. Entoprocts are predominantly

(*a*) fresh-water types
(*b*) parasitic types
(*c*) microscopic types
(*d*) creeping types along the sea floor.

Q. 809. During the contraction of a muscle

(*a*) actin and myosin molecules probably slide apart
(*b*) ATP-ase activity is probably required
(*c*) ADP in muscle is probably made into ATP
(*d*) the electrical polarization of actomyosin is probably restored.

Q. 810. A peptide link joins

(*a*) the amino groups of two amino acids
(*b*) the amino groups of one and the acid group of another amino acid
(*c*) the acid groups of two amino acids
(*d*) the amino groups of one and the peptide group of another amino acid.

Q. 811. Phosphagens release energy

(*a*) to ADP during muscle contraction
(*b*) to ATP during muscle contraction
(*c*) to ATP during muscle extension
(*d*) to ADP during muscle extension.

Q. 812. Genes function in protein synthesis as

(*a*) enzymes forming peptide links

(*b*) intermediate energy carriers
(*c*) controllers of amino acid sequences
(*d*) amino acid suppliers.

Q. 813. Light in animals

(*a*) can be produced only in discontinuous flashes
(*b*) can be produced only after nervous stimulation
(*c*) gives off a great deal of heat
(*d*) is produced only during the night or in dark places.

Q. 814. The energy for muscular contraction

(*a*) comes directly from oxygen
(*b*) appears to come from ATP breakdown
(*c*) comes directly from phosphagens
(*d*) appears to come from myosin and actin.

Q. 815. Animals can synthesize

(*a*) neither proteins nor amino acids
(*b*) some amino acids but not proteins
(*c*) proteins as well as some amino acids
(*d*) some proteins as well as all amino acids.

Q. 816. Glucose molecules can be converted to starch by

(*a*) dehydration
(*b*) dehydrogenation
(*c*) hydration
(*d*) hydrolysis.

Q. 817. Proteins are formed from amino acids by

(*a*) dehydration
(*b*) dehydrogenation
(*c*) hydration
(*d*) hydrolysis.

Q. 818. The Watson-Crick model shows how genetic-code transfer might come about between

(*a*) DNA and DNA
(*b*) DNA and RNA
(*c*) RNA and protein
(*d*) RNA and RNA.

Q. 819. Nucleoli contain

(*a*) DNA
(*b*) RNA
(*c*) both DNA and RNA
(*d*) genetic and nongenetic DNA.

Q. 820. RNA is found

(*a*) in the nucleus only
(*b*) in the cytoplasm only
(*c*) in nucleus and cytoplasm
(*d*) in molecular association with DNA only.

Q. 821. Genetic information

(*a*) never leaves the nucleus
(*b*) leaves the nucleus only during cell division
(*c*) is preserved by mutation
(*d*) is redundant.

Q. 822. Mutations are

(*a*) stable gene changes only
(*b*) errors in gene reproduction only
(*c*) radiation-induced gene changes only
(*d*) any gene changes.

Q. 823. Genetic-code transfer from DNA to RNA probably occurs

(*a*) in the chromosomes
(*b*) in the nucleoli
(*c*) in the ribosomes
(*d*) when RNA leaves the nucleus.

Q. 824. Code transcription from DNA to DNA probably occurs

(*a*) whenever transcription to RNA occurs
(*b*) only at the time of chromosome duplication
(*c*) at any time in the life cycle of a cell
(*d*) whenever proteins are synthesized in the ribosomes.

Q. 825. During anaphase of mitotic divisions

(*a*) asters disappear
(*b*) centrioles divide

(*c*) chromosomes migrate
(*d*) nuclear membranes reform.

Q. 826. Ctenophores include

(*a*) neither polymorphic nor colonial types
(*b*) both polymorphic and colonial types
(*c*) polymorphic but not colonial types
(*d*) colonial but not polymorphic types.

Q. 827. The structure of *Peripatus* strongly suggests that

(*a*) ancestral annelids used their skin for external respiration
(*b*) mollusks and annelids are closely related
(*c*) arthropods were primitively aquatic
(*d*) arthropods and annelids had a common ancestor.

Q. 828. Which of the following is found in both coelenterates and annelids?

(*a*) endoderm
(*b*) metameres
(*c*) gastrovascular cavity
(*d*) coelom.

Q. 829. Which of the following shows alternation of generations?

(*a*) crayfish
(*b*) planaria
(*c*) *Obelia*
(*d*) earthworm

Q. 830. In terms of numbers of species, the most abundant animals are

(*a*) vertebrates
(*b*) coelenterates
(*c*) echinoderms
(*d*) arthropods.

Q. 831. In the development of the eye in frog, bird, or man

(*a*) there is a cup formed from a part of the embryonic central nervous system and this cup self-differentiates to form the normal eye (*b*) there is a cup formed from a part of the embryonic central nervous system and this cup interacts with surrounding embryonic tissues to form the normal eye

(*c*) there is a cup formed from the embryonic ectoderm which joins to the embryonic nervous system by the optic nerve

(*d*) there is a cup formed from the embryonic ectoderm and this cup self-differentiates to form the normal eye.

Q. 832. A vitamin which is a steroid is

(*a*) Vitamin A
(*b*) Vitamin B_1
(*c*) Vitamin B_{12}
(*d*) Vitamin D.

Q. 833. Upon hydrolysis, proteins yield

(*a*) fatty acids
(*b*) nucleotides
(*c*) nucleic acids
(*d*) amino acids.

Q. 834. The linear array of the building blocks of protein is called

(*a*) the primary structure
(*b*) the secondary structure
(*c*) the tertiary structure
(*d*) the quaternary structure.

Q. 835. In brachiopods

(*a*) fertilization may occur in the coelom
(*b*) most species are hermaphroditic
(*c*) fertilization may occur in the gonoducts
(*d*) a drastic metamorphosis is typical.

Q. 836. Ectoprocts and entoprocts are alike in possessing

(*a*) a peritoneum
(*b*) an operculum
(*c*) an anus outside the tentacle ring
(*d*) zooids which do not exceed microscopic sizes.

Q. 837. Freshwater lophophorates comprise the class

(*a*) Gymnolaemata
(*b*) Inarticulata
(*c*) Phylactolaemata
(*d*) Articulata

Q. 838. Ectoproct larvae possess a

(*a*) pyriform organ
(*b*) nephridial pit
(*c*) pecoral lobe
(*d*) equatorial mantle fold.

Q. 839. *Balanoglossus,* the acorn worm, belongs to the phylum

(*a*) Echinodermata
(*b*) Hemichordata
(*c*) Cephalochordata
(*d*) Urochordata.

Q. 840. A compound eye is found

(*a*) in arthropods and mollusks
(*b*) in certain annelids and mollusks
(*c*) in certain annelids and arthropods
(*d*) only in arthropods.

Q. 841. A segmental architecture of the body is characteristic of annelids as well as

(*a*) arthropods and echinoderms
(*b*) vertebrates and echinoderms
(*c*) arthropods and vertebrates
(*d*) mollusks and echinoderms.

Q. 842. The vertebral column of a frog differs in the number of bones found in humans. This number is closer to

(*a*) one-half those found in humans
(*b*) one-third those found in humans
(*c*) one-eighth those found in humans
(*d*) one-tenth those found in humans.

Q. 843. One way in which frogs and men are the same in their skeletal system is

(*a*) their pelvic girdles developed from three homologous bones
(*b*) their pectoral girdles developed from three homologous bones
(*c*) their forearm bones function identifically
(*d*) they both possess a urostyle.

Q. 844. The immediate source of energy for muscle contraction is

(*a*) glycogen reduction to lactic acid
(*b*) lactic acid reduction to CO_2 and H_2O
(*c*) phosphocreatine reduction to creatine
(*d*) ATP reduction to ADP.

Q. 845. Growth of a long bone such as the humerus or femur

(*a*) occurs by addition to the end surfaces and around the shanks
(*b*) occurs by growth centers just internal to the ends of bones, and around the shanks
(*c*) occurs only by a central proliferation toward each end and around the shanks
(*d*) occurs by cartilage turning directly to bone at the ends and around the shanks.

Q. 846. The most common elements found in living systems are

(*a*) carbohydrates, fats, proteins, nucleic acids, and minerals
(*b*) carbon, hydrogen, nitrogen, and oxygen
(*c*) carbohydrates, lipids, proteins, and water
(*d*) carbon, sulfur, phosphorus, and hydrogen.

Q. 847. The denaturation of a protein is

(*a*) caused by heat or heavy metals
(*b*) the breakdown to amino acids
(*c*) its use as an enzyme
(*d*) always permanent.

Q. 848. Proteins consist entirely of

(*a*) amino acids linked together
(*b*) glycerol and fatty acids linked together
(*c*) carbon, hydrogen, and oxygen
(*d*) phosphates and glycerol.

Q. 849. Carbohydrates consist of

(*a*) amino acids linked together
(*b*) glycerol and fatty acids linked together
(*c*) carbon, hydrogen, and oxygen
(*d*) phosphates and glycerol.

Q. 850. Fats consist of

(*a*) amino acids linked together
(*b*) glycerin and fatty acids linked together
(*c*) carbon, hydrogen, oxygen, and nitrogen
(*d*) phosphates and glycerol.

Q. 851. Lipids are

(*a*) fats and sterols
(*b*) fats and proteins
(*c*) sterols and proteins, carbohydrates and sterols.
(*d*) None of these.

Q. 852. The nucleus of a cell

(*a*) does not contain DNA
(*b*) contains DNA
(*c*) contains only DNA
(*d*) does not contain RNA.

Q. 853. The endoplasmic reticulum

(*a*) permits a cell to contract
(*b*) is a network of fibrils to which chromosomes are attached
(*c*) connects one cell with another so that the cells are not loose
(*d*) is a structural component of the cell cytoplasm.

Q. 854. RNA contains

(*a*) thymine
(*b*) cytosine
(*c*) deoxyribose
(*d*) protein.

Q. 855. DNA, but not RNA, contains

(*a*) adenine
(*b*) guanine
(*c*) thymine
(*d*) cytosine.

Q. 856. In cells

(*a*) O
(*b*) H
(*c*) N
(*d*) C, occurs in the highest proportion by weight.

Q. 857. An example of a polysaccharide is

(*a*) lactose
(*b*) cellulose
(*c*) maltose
(*d*) fructose.

Q. 858. The element nitrogen is always found in

(*a*) fats
(*b*) organic compounds
(*c*) glucose
(*d*) proteins.

Q. 859. A fat consists of

(*a*) fatty acids joined
(*b*) lipids joined
(*c*) three fatty acids and glycerol joined
(*d*) three glycerol molecules and a fatty acid joined.

Q. 860. According to the cell theory

(*a*) the second law of thermodynamics has no validity
(*b*) cellular organization is the basis of life
(*c*) viruses are cells
(*d*) bacteria are not cells but organisms.

Q. 861. Ribosomes

(*a*) contain DNA
(*b*) play a role in the mechanics of cell reproduction
(*c*) are the sites of protein synthesis
(*d*) do not occur in plant cells.

Q. 862. Purines

(*a*) are components of proteins
(*b*) are certain kinds of amino acids
(*c*) have a molecular skeleton made of carbon rings
(*d*) have a molecular skeleton made of carbon-nitrogen rings.

Q. 863. Organic compounds differ from inorganic ones in their

(*a*) molecular complexity
(*b*) containing carbon atoms
(*c*) colloidal state
(*d*) occurrence in protoplasm.

Q. 864. The statocyst of ctenophores

(*a*) lies within the polar fields
(*b*) connects via fine ducts with the anal canals
(*c*) is supported by sagittal and transverse balancers
(*d*) is covered by a fused ciliary shield.

Q. 865. - The molecular changes in glycolysis result

(*a*) in the formation of two molecules of pyruvic from each glucose molecule
(*b*) in the formation of a molecule fo glucose from 2 molecules of pyruvic acid
(*c*) in the formation of lactic acid from pyruvic acid
(*d*) in the formation of 38 ATP's from ADP and inorganic phosphate.

Q. 866. The net gain of ATP's from the complete metabolism of glucose is

(*a*) 2
(*b*) 28
(*c*) 38
(*d*) 3.

Q. 867. The integrity of the active site is a function of

(*a*) the complicated folding pattern of the molecule
(*b*) a dozen or so amino acid residues which are adjacent to each other and constitute the active site

(*c*) the terminal amino acids in the protein chain
(*d*) every other amino acid residue in the protein chain.

Q. 868. Nucleic acids are composed of basic building blocks called

(*a*) nucleobases
(*b*) pyrimidines
(*c*) purines
(*d*) nucleotides.

Q. 869. The detection and assay of nucleic acids

(*a*) is impossible
(*b*) may be done only with radioactive compounds
(*c*) is a routine laboratory procedure
(*d*) is unreliable at the present time.

Q. 870. In phoronids

(*a*) the nervous system is intraepidermal
(*b*) the actinotroch larva possesses flame bulb nephridia, but the adult does not
(*c*) the lophophoral organ includes the ciliated tentacles
(*d*) the gonopores open into the brood chamber.

Q. 871. The coelom of phoronids develops

(*a*) schizocoelously
(*b*) from a mesenchymal sac
(*c*) enterocoelously
(*d*) by delamination of a tissue sheet from larval ectoderm.

Q. 872. Phoronid metamorphosis involves an eversion of the

(*a*) preoral lobe
(*b*) postoral lobe
(*c*) telotroch pouch
(*d*) metasome pouch.

Q. 873. In phoronids

(*a*) the circulatory vessels in the lophophore tentacles are open-ended
(*b*) digestion occurs intracellularly
(*c*) the sexes are largely separate

(*d*) the lophophoral tentacles near the epistome are the oldest.

Q. 874. Cleavage patterns in phornids are

(*a*) largely spiral
(*b*) largely radial
(*c*) largely bilateral
(*d*) different in different groups.

Q. 875. Actinotrochs and trochophores are alike in their

(*a*) patterns of metamorphosis
(*b*) patterns of coelom formation
(*c*) body shape
(*d*) excretory structures.

Q. 876. The outermost surface of an ectoproct is

(*a*) calcareous
(*b*) chitinous
(*c*) silicaceous
(*d*) scleroproteinaceous.

Q. 877. The polypid portion of marine ectoprocts is most highly developed in

(*a*) kenozooids
(*b*) avicularia
(*c*) vibracula
(*d*) autozooids.

Q. 878. Setiferous organs occur in

(*a*) kenozooids
(*b*) avicularia
(*c*) vibracula
(*d*) autozooids.

Q. 879. Freshwater ectoprocts do, but marine ectoprocts do not, form

(*a*) polymorphic variants
(*b*) cyphonautes larvae
(*c*) statoblasts
(*d*) hardened exoskeletons.

Q. 880. Marine ectoprocts do, but freshwater ectoprocts do not, develop

(*a*) an epistome
(*b*) statoblasts
(*c*) a horseshoe-shaped lophophore
(*d*) coelomic connections between zooids.

Q. 881. In members of the brachiopod class Inarticulata

(*a*) an anus is absent
(*b*) the lophophore is supported by skeltal props
(*c*) the valves are not interlocked but are held together muscularly
(*d*) the coelom typically develops schizocoelously.

Q. 882. In ectoprocts

(*a*) a mesocoel-metacoel septum is absent
(*b*) circulatory vessels are present
(*c*) nephridia are absent
(*d*) gonoducts are present.

Q. 883. Ectoproct brown bodies are formed from

(*a*) polypids
(*b*) cystids
(*c*) statoblasts
(*d*) funiculi.

Q. 884. Ectoproct statoblasts are

(*a*) balance receptor organs
(*b*) young larvae of freshwater genera
(*c*) polymorphic variants in a colony
(*d*) funicular growths.

Q. 885. In all brachiopods

(*a*) the anus opens into the mantle cavity
(*b*) the blood circulation is open
(*c*) the valves are interlocked posteriorly
(*d*) the peduncle (if present) leads away from the dorsal valve.

Q. 886. Organisms generally referred to as animals are not

(*a*) holotrophic
(*b*) photosynthetic
(*c*) heterotrophic
(*d*) parasitic.

Q. 887. Metamorphosis is generally taken to mean transformation of

(*a*) a zygote into an embryo
(*b*) an embryo into a larva
(*c*) a larva into an adult
(*d*) a zygote into an adult.

Q. 888. Most sessile animal groups tend to be

(*a*) headless and radially symmetrical
(*b*) headless and bilaterally symmetrical
(*c*) head-possessing and radially symmetrical
(*d*) head-possessing and bilaterally symmetrical.

Q. 889. In terms of the second law of thermodynamics, living systems are

(*a*) improbable
(*b*) stable
(*c*) disordered
(*d*) random.

Q. 890. Unspecialized cells

(*a*) are more efficient than specialized cells
(*b*) are found only among unicellular organisms
(*c*) can survive independently
(*d*) do not exist.

Q. 891. An organelle represents a level of organization

(*a*) lower than that of a compound
(*b*) higher than that of the lowest living level
(*c*) equivalent to that of a cell
(*d*) equivalent to that of a complex of compounds.

Q. 892. In many organisms, certain-cells have lost the power to

(*a*) excrete
(*b*) respire

(*c*) divide
(*d*) maintain steady states.

Q. 893. An organism is

(*a*) a collection of tissues like the stomach
(*b*) a group of similar cells
(*c*) a living unit found in nature
(*d*) anything living with a nucleus.

Q. 894. The lowest level at which matter may be said to be living is the level of the

(*a*) organism
(*b*) cell
(*c*) compound
(*d*) aggregate of compounds.

Q. 895. If the cell of a tissue are disaggregated and placed into a culture medium, the cells

(*a*) die
(*b*) do not die
(*c*) become more specialized
(*d*) form a higher level of organization.

Q. 896. Bile aids in the digestion of fats by

(*a*) lowering the surface tension
(*b*) initiating chemical breakdown
(*c*) contributing lipase
(*d*) contributing bile pigments.

Q. 897. Amylase is an enzyme which catalyzes the chemical breakdown of

(*a*) starch to maltose
(*b*) maltose to glucose
(*c*) polypeptides to amino acids
(*d*) fats to glycerol and fatty acids.

Q. 898. Peristaltic waves of contraction pass along the vertebrate small intestine

(*a*) for a few inches and die out
(*b*) and provide the only movement of the walls of that organ

(*c*) for its entire length
(*d*) but in no other part of the digestive system.

Q. 899. Bile is produced in the

(*a*) liver
(*b*) gall bladder
(*c*) bile duct
(*d*) spleen.

Q. 900. An enzyme with a wide range of substrates is

(*a*) amylase, which breakes down any protein
(*b*) lipase, which breaks down most fats
(*c*) maltase, which breaks down most sugars
(*d*) HCl, which breaks down virtually any food.

Section X

Q. 901. In mammals, absorption of fats

(*a*) takes place in the large intestine
(*b*) is primarily into the ducts of the lymphatic system
(*c*) is into the capillaries of the small intestine
(*d*) requires that they be broken down completely to fatty acids and glycerin.

Q. 902. In man, enzymes acting on proteins

(*a*) are found in saliva
(*b*) are found in the stomach
(*c*) are produced by the spleen
(*d*) are produced by the large intestine.

Q. 903. In a digestive tract, amino acids

(*a*) cannot be absorbed as such
(*b*) may result from polysaccharide digestion
(*c*) are normally broken down by pepsin
(*d*) may result from trypsis-accelerated digestion.

Q. 904. Absorption of glucose and fructose by the vertebrate small intestine

(*a*) is achieved by osmosis

(*b*) is determined by the size of the molecules
(*c*) occurs at different rates
(*d*) requires the presence of bile salts.

Q. 905. Animal carbohydrates are stored in the form of

(*a*) glucose
(*b*) glycerin
(*c*) glycogen
(*d*) glycine.

Q. 906. In mammals, urea is produced in the

(*a*) liver
(*b*) gall bladder
(*c*) kidney
(*d*) spleen.

Q. 907. In vertebrates, bile is produced in the

(*a*) liver
(*b*) gall bladder
(*c*) kidney
(*d*) spleen.

Q. 908. After leaving the mammalian digestive tract, fats go into the

(*a*) liver
(*b*) gall bladder
(*c*) lymph circulation
(*d*) blood circulation.

Q. 909. As the concentration of blood glucose tends to rise after a vertebrate eats, the concentration of liver glycogen will

(*a*) be hardly affected
(*b*) begin the fall
(*c*) begin to rise
(*d*) decrease as a result of excretion in urine.

Q. 910. The kidney of adult amphibia is

(*a*) pronephros
(*b*) nephromixium
(*c*) mesonephros
(*d*) metanephros.

Q. 911. In man, pH tends to be maintained

(*a*) at 7.0
(*b*) between 6.0 and 7.0
(*c*) between 7.0 to 8.0
(*d*) at a slightly acid level.

Q. 912. Enzymes

(*a*) provide the energy for the carrying out of a reaction
(*b*) must be supplied daily in the diet
(*c*) are protien in nature
(*d*) increase the thermal agitation of compounds.

Q. 913. An increase of 10°C in the temperature of the medium in which a chemical reaction takes place

(*a*) approximately doubles
(*b*) does not change
(*c*) roughly quadruples
(*d*) decreases two or three times, the rate at which it occurs.

Q. 914. The enzyme invertase will break down

(*a*) most sugars
(*b*) most fats
(*c*) sucrose and related sugars only
(*d*) sucrose only.

Q. 915. Enzymes participating in a chemical reaction

(*a*) are used up during the reaction
(*b*) become decomposed during the reaction
(*c*) react more rapidly as the reaction progresses
(*d*) are not consumed in the reaction.

Q. 916. Chemical reactions within cells

(*a*) cannot take place without enzymes
(*b*) are hastened by enzymes
(*c*) are not affected by enzymes
(*d*) require ions.

Q. 917. A biological community is

(*a*) made up of organisms all of which are closely related
(*b*) made up of organisms which cooperate closely with each other to insure the maximum survival of all species within the group
(*c*) made up of organisms which are adapted to the physical conditions prevailing there
(*d*) made up of organisms which live more or less independently of each other.

Q. 918. In a national park, the rangers have made a practice of systematically killing wolves, coyotes, and mountain lions. Which of the following is the most probable result of this practice?

(*a*) A number of deer reaches the optimum number characteristic of the climax condition
(*b*) There will be more deer than the area can support
(*c*) The predators will be benefited
(*d*) The aera will be characterized by little change in its flora.

Q. 919. In terms of numbers of species, the most abundant animals are

(*a*) vertebrates
(*b*) coelenterates
(*c*) echinoderms
(*d*) arthropods.

Q. 920. *Drosophila* has the following type of metamorphosis

(*a*) no metamorphosis
(*b*) gradual metamorphosis
(*c*) incomplete metamorphosis
(*d*) complete metamorphosis.

Q. 921. The crayfish possesses the following which separate it from the insects

(*a*) chitinous exoskeleton
(*b*) ten walking legs
(*c*) segmented appendages
(*d*) compound eyes.

Q. 922. Which set of organisms are all insects which are of economic and medical importance to man?

(*a*) bee, mosquito, trypanosome
(*b*) grasshopper, bee, flea, Rickettsia
(*c*) tse-tse fly, bee, grasshopper
(*d*) mosquito, tse-tse fly, *Trichonymphya.*

Q. 923. The first man to emphasize the nucleus was

(*a*) Hooke
(*b*) Schleiden
(*c*) Schwann
(*d*) Brown.

Q. 924. *Acetabularia* has been used in experiments to demonstrate

(*a*) active transport
(*b*) the role of the nucleus in metabolism
(*c*) the role of the nucleus in heredity
(*d*) the role of the nucleus in active transport.

Q. 925. Viruses range in size from

(*a*) 10 to 100 millimeters
(*b*) 10 to 100 microns
(*c*) 50 to 500 millimicrons
(*d*) 5 to 200 millimicrons.

Q. 926. A group of animal cells of like structure and origin and performing a similar function is

(*a*) an organ
(*b*) a system
(*c*) a tissue
(*d*) an organism.

Q. 927. In the basic design of the molluscan body, the longitudinal nerve cords lead off anteriorly from the

(*a*) cerebral ganglia
(*b*) pedal ganglia
(*c*) pleural ganglia
(*d*) visceral ganglia.

Q. 928. Abalones are gastropods which in larval stages undergo

(*a*) no torsion
(*b*) 180° torsion
(*c*) 90° detorsion
(*d*) 180° detorsion.

Q. 929. Gastropod structures not part of the alimentary system or not having a direct alimentary role are the

(*a*) cerata
(*b*) ctenidia
(*c*) radula
(*d*) epipodia.

Q. 930. The foot of a sea butterfly is formed into a pair of

(*a*) epipodia
(*b*) parapodia
(*c*) pteropodia
(*d*) scaphopodia.

Q. 931. Adjacent gill filaments are joined by tissue junctions

(*a*) protobranchs
(*b*) filibranchs
(*c*) culamellibranchs
(*d*) septibranchs.

Q. 932. Glochidia occur in

(*a*) freshwater clams
(*b*) terrestrial snails
(*c*) marine chitons
(*d*) bivalve mollusks in any environment.

Q. 933. Carbohydrate digestion in many clams is aided particularly by the

(*a*) hepatopancreas
(*b*) labial palps
(*c*) crystalline style
(*d*) salivary glands in the radula apparatus.

Q. 934. Between the ascending and descending parts of a clam gill lies a set of

(*a*) water tubes

(*b*) gill pores
(*c*) food grooves
(*d*) blood vessels.

Q. 935. Whelks attack prey by means of their

(*a*) byssus threads
(*b*) captacula
(*c*) tubular siphon
(*d*) radula.

Q. 936. A scaphopod possesses

(*a*) a heart
(*b*) gills
(*c*) kidneys
(*d*) a ventral operculum.

Q. 937. The sexes are separate in most

(*a*) pulmonate snails
(*b*) opisthobranch snails
(*c*) oysters
(*d*) eulamellibranch clams.

Q. 938. Telolecithal eggs and discoidal cleavage characterize the

(*a*) pulmonates
(*b*) septibranchs
(*c*) scaphopods
(*d*) cephalopods.

Q. 939. A radula is absent in

(*a*) cephalopods
(*b*) pelecypods
(*c*) gastropods
(*d*) amphineurans.

Q. 940. Captacula occur in

(*a*) mussels
(*b*) octopuses
(*c*) tusk shells
(*d*) scallops.

Q. 941. In line with the basic anatomical orientation of the mollus-can body, the head end of a squid is actually

(*a*) anterior
(*b*) dorsal
(*c*) posterior
(*d*) ventral.

Q. 942. The all-or-none law says

(*a*) a minimal stimuls causes a complete contraction of a muscle fiber or an impulse to pass throughout a neuron
(*b*) all the muscle fibers of a muscle contract when one is stimulated
(*c*) all the nerve fibers of a nerve have identical electrical patterns at the same time
(*d*) all the cranial nerves must be intact for the brain to function.

Q. 943. One of the functions of the Schwann sheath is

(*a*) to carry messages away from the cell body
(*b*) to carry messages to the cell body
(*c*) to slow down nerve impulses
(*d*) to provide a pathway for axon regeneration.

Q. 944. Which of the following would not be classified as a purely reflex response?

(*a*) breathing
(*b*) digestion
(*c*) walking
(*d*) knee jerk.

Q. 945. During anaphase of mitotic divisions

(*a*) asters disappear
(*b*) centrioles divide
(*c*) chromosomes migrate
(*d*) nuclear membranes reform.

Q. 946. In most animals, sexuality is a response to

(*a*) a good food supply

(*b*) periods of stress
(*c*) hormones
(*d*) unicellularity.

Q. 947. Sexuality has adaptive value because it

(*a*) insures the continued existence of various species
(*b*). produces new genetic combinations
(*c*) allows for a greater rate of reproduction
(*d*) makes mating possible.

Q. 948. The testes of mammals

(*a*) are inside the body
(*b*) outside the body
(*c*) nonfunctional during the breeding season
(*d*) differently located in different species.

Q. 949. In vegetative reproduction, a new individual is produced by

(*a*) the union of two gametes
(*b*) cell division
(*c*) a zygote
(*d*) a spore.

Q. 950. During conjugation in *Paramecium*

(*a*) nuclei are exchanged
(*b*) reproduction occurs
(*c*) nuclei are discarded
(*d*) two cells of the same mating type unite sexually.

Q. 951. Vegetative reproduction

(*a*) is not encountered among animals
(*b*) is always a result of injury to the parent
(*c*) occurs quite often among multicellular animals
(*d*) usually involves the formation of colonies.

Q. 952. Fertilization

(*a*) is always an essential requirement
(*b*) does not occur in hermaphroditism
(*c*) occurs in gametic reproduction only
(*d*) occurs only rarely in self-fertilizing hermaphrodites.

Q. 953. In an animal in which the diploid chromosome number is four, the chromosome number of each gamete will be

(*a*) eight
(*b*) four
(*c*) two
(*d*) one.

Q. 954. The zygote which produced you received

(*a*) all its chromosomes from your mother
(*b*) all its chromosomes from your father
(*c*) half its chromosomes from your mother, half from your father
(*d*) a random number of chromosomes from your mother, the rest from your father.

Q. 955. In multicellular animals, reproduction of the whole animal

(*a*) may occur by mitotic division alone
(*b*) requires mitotic as well as meiotic division
(*c*) may occur by meiotic division alone
(*d*) requires at least meiotic divisions in all cases.

Q. 956. Animals in which one gamete type is motile and the other gamete type is nonmotile are said to be

(*a*) isogamous
(*b*) anisogamous
(*c*) oögamous
(*d*) hermaphroditic.

Q. 957. Estrogenic hormones cause the

(*a*) secondary sex characteristics of the male to develop
(*b*) mammary glands to produce milk
(*c*) oviducts to be maintained
(*d*) sperm to form in the testes.

Q. 958. Estrogen in vertebrates is secreted by the

(*a*) cells of the testes
(*b*) anterior lobe of the pituitary gland
(*c*) cells of the follicle
(*d*) corpus luteum.

Q. 959. An alkali is any substance which

(*a*) dissociates in water
(*b*) gives off hydroxyl ions
(*c*) gives off hydrogen ions
(*d*) has a pH of less than 7.

Q. 960. The mechanism by which enzymes act

(*a*) involves breakdown of the enzyme
(*b*) does not involve the enzyme in the reaction
(*c*) is by temporary combination with the reactants
(*d*) is by less of specificity.

Q. 961. A reacting system will be most stable if

(*a*) enthalpy and entropy are at a maximum
(*b*) enthalpy and entropy are at a mimimum
(*c*) enthaply is greatest and entropy is least
(*d*) enthalpy is least and entropy is greatest.

Q. 962. At equilibrium, the Δ F of a reaction is numerically

(*a*) positive
(*b*) negative
(*c*) zero
(*d*) variable, depending on the nature of the particular reaction.

Q. 963. Chelicerate arthropods differ from mandibulate arthropods in that they

(*a*) have only one pair of antennae
(*b*) may have one or two pair of antennae
(*c*) lack antennae
(*d*) often have a cephalothorax.

Q. 964. Arthropods differ from annelids in possessing

(*a*) a chitinous endoskeleton
(*b*) a chitinous exoskeleton
(*c*) a circulatory system
(*d*) an excretory system.

Q. 965. The following is an arthropod excretory structure

(*a*) sinus gland

(b) Malpighian tubules
(c) X-organ
(d) antennule.

Q. 966. In chelicerate arthropods the cephalothorax typically bears how many pairs of appendages?

(a) 2
(b) 3
(c) 4
(d) 6.

Q. 967. The synthesis of maltose, a disaccharide, involves

(a) the union of two glucose molecules with the elimination of a molecule of water
(b) the breakdown of trisaccharides
(c) the glucose molecules with the addition of a molecule of water
(d) None of these

Q. 968. Cellulose is

(a) a carbohydrate
(b) a protein
(c) a nucleic acid
(d) a lipid.

Q. 969. The true fats

(a) contain C, H and O with H and O present in the same proportions as in water
(b) B contain C, H and O with O not present in the same proportions as in water
(c) are fatty acids
(d) are phospholipids.

Q. 970. The unsaturated fatty acids

(a) contain some double bonds between carbon atoms
(b) are phospholipids
(c) are steroids
(d) are the true fats.

Q. 971. Development of freshwater clams is characterized particularly by

(*a*) absence of larval stages
(*b*) trochophores
(*c*) veligers
(*d*) glochidia.

Q. 972. Development of squids is characterized particularly by

(*a*) absence of larval stages
(*b*) trochophores
(*c*) veligers
(*d*) glochidia.

Q. 973. A gill heart in squids pumps

(*a*) arterial blood from a gill
(*b*) venous blood into a gill
(*c*) arterial blood into a gill
(*d*) venous blood from a gill.

Q. 974. In cephalopods, sepermatophores are frequently transferred from male to female by the

(*a*) siphuncle
(*b*) funnel
(*c*) hectocotylus
(*d*) genital papilla.

Q. 975. The chambered *Nautilus* possesses

(*a*) two pairs of ctenidia
(*b*) a closed circulation
(*c*) an ink sac
(*d*) sucker-equipped tentacles.

Q. 976. The mammalian homologue of the kidney of the frog

(*a*) gives rise to the epididymis in the male, nothing functional in the female
(*b*) functional tubules in males and females
(*c*) Cowper's gland
(*d*) is the uterus produced by fusion of mesonephric ducts.

Q. 977. In the passage of gametes from their origin

(*a*) neither eggs nor sperm enter the bladder

(*b*) sperm enter the bladder
(*c*) eggs, after fertilization, pass from the bladder to the uterus
(*d*) both eggs and sperm travel by homologus ducts which by-pass the bladder.

Q. 978. It is incorrect to say that the anterior pituitary lobe is the source of

(*a*) growth stimulating hormone, prolactin, adrenocorticotropic
(*b*) thyrotropin, FSH, ACTH
(*c*) FSH, adrenocorticotropic, growth stimulating hormone
(*d*) ACTH, prolactin, progesterone.

Q. 979. The essential element incorporated into the production of the hormone of the thyroid gland is

(*a*) iron
(*b*) iodine
(*c*) calcium
(*d*) sodium.

Q. 980. Synthesis reactions are commonly characterized by

(*a*) equilibrium constants smaller than one
(*b*) positive Δ Fs
(*c*) low activation-energy requirements
(*d*) high energy yields.

Q. 981. In general, cofactor may act by

(*a*) attaching to an active site of an enzyme
(*b*) attaching to a part of an enzyme which is not an active site
(*c*) functioning as the specific substrate of an enzyme
(*d*) increasing the collision rate among the substrate molecules.

Q. 982. A scientific law is a well-substantiated

(*a*) experiment
(*b*) hypothesis
(*c*) theory
(*d*) observation.

Q. 983. Zoological science contains

(*a*) both pure and applied phases
(*b*) more pure than applied phases
(*c*) more applied than pure phases
(*d*) pure phases only.

Q. 984. Science is not

(*a*) a system of communication
(*b*) a method of investigation
(*c*) a philosophy of life
(*d*) an outgrowth of tribal magic.

Q. 985. The function of controls in experimentation is to

(*a*) prevent errors
(*b*) make the evidence certain
(*c*) ensure that a clear "yes" or "no" answer is obtained
(*d*) provide a frame of reference for judging results.

Q. 986. The best scientific work is always done

(*a*) artistically
(*b*) unemotionally
(*c*) without thought of possible practical advantages
(*d*) in response to practical needs.

Q. 987. The argument that ancestral frogs wanted to live on land and that they therefore shed their gills and developed lungs is an example of

(*a*) causalism
(*b*) materialism
(*c*) teleology
(*d*) mechanism.

Q. 988. Modern zoology is predominantly

(*a*) causalistic
(*b*) vitalistic
(*c*) teleological
(*d*) antireligious.

Q. 989. An externally segmented body is characteristic of

(*a*) archiannelids and earthworms

(*b*) tardigrades and leeches
(*c*) *Peripatus* and pentastomids
(*d*) echiuroids and lugworms.

Q. 990. In burrowing polychaetes, the pharynx is

(*a*) eversible and unarmed
(*b*) not eversible and unarmed
(*c*) eversible and armed
(*d*) not eversible and armed.

Q. 991. Archiannelids are

(*a*) hermaphroditic
(*b*) without parapodia
(*c*) unsegmented internally
(*d*) equipped with metanephridia or nephromixia.

Q. 992. Among the excretory devices of earthworms are

(*a*) typhlosoles
(*b*) solenocytes
(*c*) micronephridia
(*d*) chloragogues.

Q. 993. Internal segmentation of the adults is characteristic

(*a*) echiuroids and sipunculids
(*b*) echiuroids but not sipunculids
(*c*) sipunculids but not echiuroids
(*d*) neither echiuroids nor sipunculids.

Q. 994. Tardigrades develop

(*a*) via trochophore larvae
(*b*) metanephridial excretory systems
(*c*) endodermal coelom sacs
(*d*) tracheal breathing systems.

Q. 995. Pentastomids are parasitic

(*a*) as larvae and as adults
(*b*) as larvae but not as adults
(*c*) as adults but not as larvae
(*d*) only during the molting periods of the larval phase.

Q. 996. The structure of *Peripatus* suggests strongly that

(*a*) ancestral annelids breathed through their skins
(*b*) mollusks and annelids are closely related
(*c*) arthropods were primitively aquatic
(*d*) arthropods have evolved from annelid stock.

Q. 997. A trochophore larva does not occur in the development of

(*a*) echiuroids
(*b*) sipunculids
(*c*) archiannelids
(*d*) pentastomids.

Q. 998. The prostomium of *Nereis*

(*a*) bears the mouth
(*b*) bears four pairs of tentacular palps
(*c*) is without appendages
(*d*) represents the head.

Q. 999. In *Nereis*

(*a*) paired lateral vessels in posterior trunk segments function as hearts
(*b*) the nephrostomes of one segment open into the anteriorly adjacent segment
(*c*) gonoducts exit near the nephridiopores
(*d*) the cerebral ganglia lie in the peristonmium.

Q. 1000. Animals at the top of a food chain

(*a*) breed faster than those lower in the food chain
(*b*) are smaller than those lower in the chain
(*c*) are more numerous than those lower in the chain
(*d*) are carnivorous.

Section XI

Q. 1001. The climate of the grassland region differs from that of a forest region in that the grassland receives less

(*a*) moisture
(*b*) light

(*c*) wind
(*d*) extremes of temperature.

Q. 1002. The climax stage of a biotic succession

(*a*) persists until the environment or climate changes
(*b*) changes rapidly from time to time
(*c*) is the first stage in a succession
(*d*) is the stage in which only plants are present.

Q. 1003. Ancestors of modern scorpions were probably

(*a*) the eurypterids
(*b*) the trilobite larva
(*c*) *Limulus*
(*d*) pycnogonids.

Q. 1004. The largest arthropods ever known were

(*a*) ammonites
(*b*) eurypterids
(*c*) king crabs
(*d*) ancient dragonflies.

Q. 1005. Pycnogonids are

(*a*) terrestrial
(*b*) fresh water
(*c*) terrestrial and fresh water
(*d*) marine.

Q. 1006. Poison fangs are characteristic of

(*a*) all spiders
(*b*) the black widow spider and closely related species
(*c*) only a few subfamilies of spiders
(*d*) black widows and tarantulas only.

Q. 1007. Hemoglobin has which components?

(*a*) 2 α-and 2 β-chains
(*b*) 1 α-and 2 β-chains
(*c*) 2 α-and 1 β-chains
(*d*) 1 α-and 1 β-chains

Q. 1008. Of the enzymes which are conjugated proteins the protein moiety of the molecule is called the

(*a*) apoenzyme
(*b*) holoenzyme
(*c*) coenzyme
(*d*) the prosthetic group.

Q. 1009. Niacin

(*a*) prevents beriberi
(*b*) is a member of the water soluble group of vitamins
(*c*) was discovered by Eijkman
(*d*) is found chiefly in corn.

Q. 1010. Which of the following is not one of the six categories of foods?

(*a*) water
(*b*) inorganic salts
(*c*) lipids
(*d*) none of the above.

Q. 1011. In mammals, fertilization usually takes place in the

(*a*) ovary
(*b*) uterus
(*c*) vagina
(*d*) oviduct.

Q. 1012. Progesterone in mammals stimulates the

(*a*) mammary glands to secrete milk
(*b*) follicle to rupture from the ovary
(*c*) lining of the uterus to break down
(*d*) development of the placenta.

Q. 1013. The lactogenic hormone of mammals stimulates the

(*a*) corpus luteum to secrete
(*b*) mammary glands to form milk
(*c*) lining of the uterus to thicken
(*d*) secondary sexual characteristics to develop.

Q. 1014. The menstrual cycle is characteristic of man and

(*a*) rabbits, squirels, and other rodents
(*b*) all other mammals
(*c*) rabbits and cats
(*d*) apes and some monkeys.

Q. 1015. The hormone progesterone which maintains the lining of the mammalian uterus during pregnancy is secreted by

(*a*) cells of the testis
(*b*) the follicle in the ovary
(*c*) the corpus luteum in the ovary
(*d*) the pituitary glands.

Q. 1016. The secondary sexual characters of male mammals are under the direct control of

(*a*) FSH
(*b*) LH
(*c*) estrogen
(*d*) testosterone.

Q. 1017. In many animals, eggs are produced which normally develop without being fertilized and give rise to normal adults without male parents. This process is called

(*a*) parturition
(*b*) gestation
(*c*) parthenogenesis
(*d*) hermaphroditism.

Q. 1018. Secondary sex characteristics in female vertebrates are maintained by

(*a*) anderogens
(*b*) estrogens
(*c*) gonadotropic hormones
(*d*) progesterone.

Q. 1019. Testosterone is a vertebrate hormone secreted by the

(*a*) interstitial cells of the testes
(*b*) follicle
(*c*) corpus luteum
(*d*) anterior lobe of the pituitary gland.

Q. 1020. The estrogenic hormones are secreted by

(*a*) an anterior lobe of the pituitary
(*b*) the posterior lobe of the pituitary
(*c*) the follicle
(*d*) the corpus luteum.

Q. 1021. Testosterone

(*a*) makes females receptive to males
(*b*) prepares the mammary glands for secretion
(*c*) reduces secondary sexual characteristics
(*d*) maintains the ducts leading from the testes.

Q. 1022. The luteinizing hormone (LH)

(*a*) stimulates corpus luteum formation
(*b*) stimulates corpus luteum secretion
(*c*) stimulates follicle formation
(*d*) is absent in male vertebrates.

Q. 1023. The follicle stimulating hormone (FSH) of vertebrates

(*a*) is secreted by the ovary
(*b*) has no effect in the male
(*c*) has no effect in the female
(*d*) causes the follicle to develop in the female and sperm to develop in the male.

Q. 1024. The hormone progesterone of man

(*a*) affects only the uterus
(*b*) affects only the ducts of the testis
(*c*) affects the mammary glands
(*d*) causes growth of the follicle.

Q. 1025. A menstrual cycle

(*a*) occurs several times a year
(*b*) is seasonal in nature
(*c*) occurs in all mammals
(*d*) occurs in man only.

Q. 1026. Ovulation is the process by which

(*a*) sperms are ejected from the gonopore
(*b*) an egg is ejected from the ovary
(*c*) an egg implants on the wall of the uterus
(*d*) an egg is produced and brought to maturity.

Q. 1027. The umbilical cord of placental mammals contains portions of the

(*a*) sperm duct

(*b*) ammion
(*c*) allantois
(*d*) chorion.

Q. 1028. In birds, the allantois is pressed against the inner surface of the shell and functions

(*a*) as an outlet for egested matter
(*b*) as a lung in gas
(*c*) as a lung in surface
(*d*) None of these.

Q. 1029. The aim of science is

(*a*) to uncover facts
(*b*) to construct theories
(*c*) to discover truth
(*d*) to prove reality.

Q. 1030. A well planned scientific experiment is designed to

(*a*) test an observation
(*b*) test a hypothesis
(*c*) prove that something is true
(*d*) provide controlled facts.

Q. 1031. A hypothesis can be defined as

(*a*) a likely answer to a question based on certain observations
(*b*) a conclusion reached from a group of theories
(*c*) a law of limited application
(*d*) a central fact derived from a number of experiments.

Q. 1032. A scientific theory is

(*a*) a law which has not been proved conclusively
(*b*) an extension of experimental evidence
(*c*) a prediction unsupported by evidence
(*d*) a statement of a natural law.

Q. 1033. In a controlled experiment, the control series and the experimental series of tests

(*a*) are identical in all respects
(*b*) are identical in all respects except one

(*c*) are not identical except in one respect
(*d*) are not identical in any respect.

Q. 1034. Mitochondria

(*a*) are large ribosomes
(*b*) are small nucleoli
(*c*) are centers for organized catabolic processes
(*d*) are peculiar to plant cells.

Q. 1035. Diffusion only takes place

(*a*) across semipermeable membranes
(*b*) in true solutions
(*c*) in living cells
(*d*) in the presence of concentration differences.

Q. 1036. The endoplasmic reticulum often has subcellular structures attached to it which are called

(*a*) mitochondria
(*b*) Golgi bodies
(*c*) ribosomes
(*d*) desmosomes.

Q. 1037. The net osmotic difference would be greatest between cytoplasm and

(*a*) 0.9% NaCl solution
(*b*) distilled water
(*c*) blood or sap
(*d*) pond water.

Q. 1038. Golgi bodies in cells appear to function in

(*a*) gene control
(*b*) cell division
(*c*) secretion
(*d*) RNA synthesis.

Q. 1039. The crop of earthworms

(*a*) absorbs calcium into the blood circulation
(*b*) excretes calcium from the blood circulation
(*c*) stores ingested material
(*d*) grinds swallowed earth.

Q. 1040. The dorsal blood vessel in earthworms

(*a*) is reduced or absent
(*b*) possess valves
(*c*) carries blood posteriorly
(*d*) is contractile.

Q. 1041. Male gonopores in earthworms are situated in segment

(*a*) 9
(*b*) 11
(*c*) 13
(*d*) 15.

Q. 1042. The receptacles in segments 9 and 10 of an earthworm store

(*a*) sperms of that worm
(*b*) eggs of that worm
(*c*) sperms of a mating partner
(*d*) eggs of a mating partner.

Q. 1043. Leeches

(*a*) generally do not possess a clitellum
(*b*) develop an increasing number of segments during adult life
(*c*) usually are without setae
(*d*) typically possess anterior and midventral suckers, like flukes.

Q. 1044. Oligochaetes do, but polychaetes do not, possess

(*a*) subneural blood vessels
(*b*) eyes
(*c*) notopodial setae
(*d*) nonchitinous cuticles.

Q. 1045. Polychaetes are, but oligochaetes are not, characterized by

(*a*) prostomial appendages
(*b*) typhlosoles
(*c*) spiral cleavage
(*d*) intersegmental septa.

Q. 1046. The coelom of sipunculids contains

(*a*) red blood cells,
(*b*) debris-collecting nuchal organs
(*c*) fibrous connective tissue
(*d*) segmental septa

Q. 1047. Echiuroids include the genus

(*a*) *Sabella*
(*b*) *Arenicola*
(*c*) *Bonellia*
(*d*) *Linguatula.*

Q. 1048. The ratio of H:O in a molecule of carbohydrate is

(*a*) 2:1
(*b*) 1:2
(*c*) variable
(*d*) the same as the ratio of C:O.

Q. 1049. A mass of cytoplasm with nuclei in it which are not separated by cell membranes is known as a

(*a*) synergism
(*b*) syllogism
(*c*) syncytium
(*d*) symbiosis.

Q. 1050. A cell may be defined as

(*a*) any mass of cytoplasm with a cell wall
(*b*) any mass of cytoplasm with a cell membrane
(*c*) any protozoan
(*d*) a nucleus with cytoplasm.

Q. 1051. Glycogen consists of

(*a*) one simple sugar molecule
(*b*) glucose molecules linked by loss of water
(*c*) maltose and fructose linked
(*d*) glucose and fructose linked.

. 1052. The primary structure of a protein is maintained by

(*a*) peptide bonds

(*b*) hydrogen bonds
(*c*) disulfide bonds
(*d*) ionic bonds.

Q. 1053. The fibril connecting a basal granule and a centriole is known as the

(*a*) kinetosome
(*b*) mastigoneme
(*c*) rhizoplast
(*d*) blepharoplast.

Q. 1054. Glucose is a

(*a*) ketopentose
(*b*) aldohexose
(*c*) ketoheptose
(*d*) aldopentose.

Q. 1055. An example of a nucleotide is

(*a*) deoxyribose
(*b*) cytosine
(*c*) nicotinic acid
(*d*) adenylic acid.

Q. 1056. When the presence or absence of a physical or biotic factor determines the presence or absence of a certain organism, this factor is termed

(*a*) an ecological equivalent of the organism
(*b*) a limiting factor of the organism
(*c*) an ecological interrelationship of the organism
(*d*) a principle of cooperation.

Q. 1057. A primary consumer is characterized by which one of the following?

(*a*) it is a plant possessing chlorophyll
(*b*) it is a vegetarian
(*c*) it is a predator
(*d*) it is of relatively large size.

Q. 1058. Which of the following organisms is most numerous in the open ocean?

(*a*) blue-green algae
(*b*) fungi
(*c*) brown algae
(*d*) diatoms.

Q. 1059. If the following organism constitute a food chain, which organism would be at the top or apex of the so-called pyramid of numbers?

(*a*) hawk
(*b*) fox
(*c*) corn plant
(*d*) mouse.

Q. 1060. The competitors of carnivores are

(*a*) other carnivores
(*b*) herbivores
(*c*) other animals of the same size
(*d*) none of the above types of animals.

Q. 1061. Chelicerates which are vectors of serious diseases are found in the order

(*a*) Araneae
(*b*) Scorpionida
(*c*) Acarina
(*d*) Solpugida.

Q. 1062. The pycnogonid abdomen is

(*a*) six segmented
(*b*) absent
(*c*) provided with a potent stinger
(*d*) minute and unsegmented.

Q. 1063. The largest class in the subphylum Chelicerata is the class

(*a*) Scorpionida
(*b*) Araneae
(*c*) Arachnida
(*d*) Acarina.

Q. 1064. Structures called pectines on the scorpion abdomen are probably

(*a*) chemoreceptors
(*b*) thermal receptors
(*c*) tactile receptors
(*d*) accessory excretory organs.

Q. 1065. The movement of substances through living cell membranes where energy is required is usually

(*a*) impossible
(*b*) very slow
(*c*) by osmosis
(*d*) by active transport.

Q. 1066. The third embryonic segment of chelicerates typically bears

(*a*) pedipalps
(*b*) walking legs
(*c*) chelicerae
(*d*) no appendages.

Q. 1067. Compound eyes are (or were) not present in

(*a*) trilobites
(*b*) *Limulus*
(*c*) eurypterids
(*d*) arachnids.

Q. 1068. The pectines of scorpions are

(*a*) breathing structures
(*b*) borne on the first abdominal segment
(*c*) homologous to gill books
(*d*) sound receptors.

Q. 1069. The basal endite of a segmental appendage in arthropods is the

(*a*) epipodite
(*b*) basipodite
(*c*) endopodite
(*d*) coxopodite.

Q. 1070. Horsehoe crabs excrete via

(*a*) Malpighian tubules

(*b*) green glands
(*c*) coxal glands
(*d*) chilaria.

Q. 1071. The segmental structure of eurypterids was most nearly like that of

(*a*) spiders
(*b*) sea spiders
(*c*) horseshoe crabs
(*d*) scorpions.

Q. 1072. Malpighian tubules communicate with the

(*a*) exterior through separate openings
(*b*) cloaca or rectum
(*c*) midgut
(*d*) hindgut.

Q. 1073. Breathing structures known to occur together in a single individual of certain chelicerates are

(*a*) gill books and lung books
(*b*) lung books and tracheae
(*c*) gill books and tracheae
(*d*) tracheae and ostia.

Q. 1074. Among chelicerates, seven pairs of cephalothoracic appendages are present in

(*a*) horseshoe crabs
(*b*) eurypterids
(*c*) scorpions
(*d*) spiders.

Q. 1075. Among chelicerates, uniramous appendages typically occur in

(*a*) both cephalothorax and abdomen
(*b*) cephalothorax only
(*c*) abdomen only
(*d*) neither cephalothorax nor abdomen.

Q. 1076. The developing human egg becomes buried in the lining of the uterus, a process called

(*a*) invagination
(*b*) internalization
(*c*) implantation
(*d*) placentation.

Q. 1077. In its passage through an oviduct, a fertilized egg

(*a*) swims by itself
(*b*) descends by gravity
(*c*) is propelled by cilia
(*d*) moves through peristalsis.

Q. 1078. Vertebrate LH stimulates

(*a*) the sperm ducts of the testes
(*b*) the pituitary
(*c*) the follicle to rupture
(*d*) the corpus luteum.

Q. 1079. In placental mammals, the yolk sac

(*a*) is a vestigial structure without demonstrable function
(*b*) serves as in birds for the storage of yolk
(*c*) serves as a shock absorber for the embryo
(*d*) is not formed.

Q. 1080. Progesterone is produced by

(*a*) the pituitary
(*b*) the testis
(*c*) the corpus luteum
(*d*) the follicle.

Q. 1081. A placenta is region where

(*a*) maternal and embryonic blood mix
(*b*) embryonic blood gives off oxygen
(*c*) maternal blood receives carbon dioxide
(*d*) embryonic blood is produced.

Q. 1082. LH is

(*a*) a polysaccharide
(*b*) a tetrapyrrol
(*c*) a sterol
(*d*) a protein.

Q. 1083. Aside from its importance in restoring the characteristic chromosome number of the species, penetration of an egg by a sperm is significant in that it

(*a*) brings in a large amount of cytoplasm contributed by male parent
(*b*) makes an opening in the egg through which accumulated wastes are ejected
(*c*) stimulates the egg to prepare for the first cleavage divison
(*d*) completes the fertilization process.

Q. 1084. Fertilization is accomplished when

(*a*) the sperm has enetred the egg
(*b*) egg and sperm nuclei have fused
(*c*) a fertilization membrane has formed around the egg
(*d*) a mature sperm meets a mature egg.

Q. 1085. The birth process in man involves the rupturing of the

(*a*) yolk sac
(*b*) amnion
(*c*) uterus
(*d*) allantois.

Q. 1086. The amnion is a fluid-filled bag which functions to

(*a*) cushion the embryo against shocks
(*b*) protect the embryo from light
(*c*) carry nutrients from surrounding tissue into the embryo proper
(*d*) participate in placenta formation.

Q. 1087. The discharge in menstruation contains

(*a*) the unfertilized egg
(*b*) the zygote
(*c*) a portion of the placenta
(*d*) a portion of the uterine lining.

Q. 1088. The acrosome of a sperm is

(*a*) a conspicuous component of the middle piece
(*b*) at the base of the sperm tail

(*c*) at the tip of the sperm head
(*d*) the only remnants of the original cytoplasm.

Q. 1089. One of the early steps in the formation of both eggs and sperms is

(*a*) conjugation
(*b*) yolk accumulation
(*c*) polar body formation
(*d*) pairing of chromosomes.

Q. 1090. A mature egg usually does not possess

(*a*) cytoplasm
(*b*) chromatin material
(*c*) stored food
(*d*) motility.

Q. 1091. Only external fertilization occurs in the gametic reproduction of animals which are

(*a*) aquatic
(*b*) sessile
(*c*) terrestrial
(*d*) motile.

Q. 1092. The most widespread form of vegetative reproduction is

(*a*) binary fission
(*b*) budding
(*c*) multiple fission
(*d*) fragmentation.

Q. 1093. Seminal fluid is secreted by

(*a*) seminal receptacles
(*b*) shell glands
(*c*) sperm sacs
(*d*) prostate glands.

Q. 1094. The extra-embryonic membrane that encloses the embryo in a fluid-filled sac is

(*a*) non-existent
(*b*) amnion
(*c*) chorion
(*d*) allantois.

Q. 1095. The extra-embryonic membrane in the human that contacts the uterine wall first is

(*a*) albumen
(*b*) amnion
(*c*) allantois
(*d*) chorion.

Q. 1096. The primitive streak of birds and mammals is homologous with the frog's

(*a*) archenteron
(*b*) area pellucida
(*c*) blastopore
(*d*) area opaca.

Q. 1097. Low thyroid output in the newborn can lead to the production of

(*a*) cretinism
(*b*) acnondroplastic dwarfism
(*c*) acromegaly
(*d*) Addison's disease.

Q. 1098. An organ of doubtful endocrine function until recently when evidence accumulated for its role in stimulating lymphocyte production is

(*a*) testis
(*b*) kidney
(*c*) stomach
(*d*) thymus.

Q. 1099. The organ which seems to be most closely associated with the function of the sympathetic nervous system is

(*a*) anterior lobe of pituitary
(*b*) posterior lobe of pituitary
(*c*) islets of Langerhans
(*d*) medulla of the adrenal.

Q. 1100. Spiders represent

(*a*) an arachnid class
(*b*) a chelicerate class

(*c*) an arachnid order
(*d*) a chelicerate order.

Section XII

Q. 1101. **Chelicerates are distinguished from other arthropods most sharply by the**

(*a*) presence of an unsegmented cephalothorax
(*b*) absence of abdominal walking legs
(*c*) presence of a telson
(*d*) absence of biting structures in the mouth.

Q. 1102. **An exoskeletal plate of an arthropod segment is referred to generally as a(n)**

(*a*) operculum
(*b*) sclerite
(*c*) pygidium
(*d*) endite.

Q. 1103. **The principal nitrogenous waste excreted by terrestrial arthropods is**

(*a*) urea
(*b*) ammonia
(*c*) uracil
(*d*) uric acid.

Q. 1104. **The characteristic pattern of arthropod development includes**

(*a*) telolecithal eggs and spiral cleavage
(*b*) telolecithal eggs and superficial cleavage
(*c*) centrolecithal eggs and spiral cleavage
(*d*) centrolecithal eggs and superficial cleavage.

Q. 1105. **Arthropods are characterized by the absence of**

(*a*) cilia
(*b*) segmental coeloms
(*c*) specific cleavage patterns
(*d*) free-living larvae.

Q. 1106. Horseshoe crabs and sea spiders are alike in that both groups possess

(*a*) ovigerous legs
(*b*) seven pairs of cephalothoracic appendages
(*c*) chilaria
(*d*) opercula.

Q. 1107. Horseshoe crabs and scorpions are alike in that both groups possess

(*a*) ovigerous legs
(*b*) seven pairs of cephalothoracic appendages
(*c*) chilaria
(*d*) opercula.

Q. 1108. As a group, spiders are distinguished from other arachnids in that they possess

(*a*) an unsegmented cephalothorax and abdomen
(*b*) ocelli only, i.e., not compound eyes
(*c*) lung books
(*d*) pedipalps, which are leglike and tactile.

Q. 1109. Arachnids differ from other chelicerates in that they are largely

(*a*) carnivorous
(*b*) terrestrial
(*c*) without jaws
(*d*) without compound eyes.

Q. 1110. The center for the sense of hearing is localized in the

(*a*) temporal lobe
(*b*) olfactory lobe
(*c*) medulla
(*d*) thalamus.

Q. 1111. The internal organs of vertebrates, such as the stomach, intestine, bladder and heart are under the control of the

(*a*) cerebrum
(*b*) cord
(*c*) peripheral nerves
(*d*) autonomic nervous system.

Q. 1112. When the dorsal fiber bundle of a spinal nerve is cut

(*a*) the organism dies
(*b*) sensation is lost in the structures which that nerve innervates
(*c*) ability to move is lost
(*d*) the ventral fiber bundle takes over functionally.

Q. 1113. The principal absorptive organ in the alimentary system of a lobster is the

(*a*) gastric mill
(*b*) foregut
(*c*) hepatopancreas
(*d*) filtering compartment of the stomach.

Q. 1114. The principal functions of the sinus glands of lobsters are

(*a*) endocrine
(*b*) excretory
(*c*) statoreceptive
(*d*) chemoreceptive.

Q. 1115. In crustacean larvae, excretion takes place primarily in

(*a*) maxillary glands
(*b*) prothoracic glands
(*c*) antennal glands
(*d*) sinus glands.

Q. 1116. Fairy shrimps and brine shrimps are members of the subclass

(*a*) Branchiopoda
(*b*) Copepoda
(*c*) Cirripedia
(*d*) Malacostraca.

Q. 1117. Millipedes form the class

(*a*) Chilopoda
(*b*) Symphyla
(*c*) Diplopoda
(*d*) Pauropoda.

Q. 1118. Posteriorly located gonopores are characteristic of

(*a*) centipedes
(*b*) millipedes
(*c*) pauropods
(*d*) symphylans

Q. 1119. Millipedes

(*a*) can run faster than centipedes
(*b*) possess two pairs of legs on each trunk segment
(*c*) are herbivorous
(*d*) are eyeless.

Q. 1120. The largest number of known insect species belongs to the order

(*a*) Diptera
(*b*) Lepidoptera
(*c*) Coleoptera
(*d*) Hymenoptera.

Q. 1121. In a housefly, the proboscis which guides the sucking apparatus is formed from the

(*a*) maxillae
(*b*) labium
(*c*) epipharynx
(*d*) hypopharynx.

Q. 1122. If a caterpillar has biting and chewing mouth parts, the later adult could be a

(*a*) cricket
(*b*) beetle
(*c*) ear wig
(*d*) dragon fly.

Q. 1123. In a nauplius larva, appendages are present on head segments

(*a*) 1, 2 and 3
(*b*) 2, 3 and 4
(*c*) 2, 3, 4, and 5
(*d*) 2, 3, 4, 5, and 6.

Q. 1124. In a lobster, chelate limbs are present on thoracic segments

(*a*) 1
(*b*) 4
(*c*) 4 through 8
(*d*) 1 through 5.

Q. 1125. The labium of insects is homologous to the crustacean

(*a*) first maxilae
(*b*) first maxillipeds
(*c*) second maxillae
(*d*) second maxillipeds.

Q. 1126. In all mandibulates, the fourth head segment bears

(*a*) antennae
(*b*) mandibles
(*c*) a labrum
(*d*) maxillae.

Q. 1127. In crustacea, blood enters the heart via the

(*a*) ostia
(*b*) open end of the posterior dorsal vessel
(*c*) sternal vessels
(*d*) atria.

Q. 1128. Scyphomedusae mature directly fro free-swimming

(*a*) planula larvae
(*b*) scyphistoma larvae
(*c*) actinula larvae
(*d*) ephyra larvae.

Q. 1129. Which concept is *not* part of the cell theory?

(*a*) Cells are the unit of structure of living things
(*b*) All cells are genetically identical
(*c*) All cells arise from pre-existing cells
(*d*) Cells are the unit of function of living things.

Q. 1130. In a compound microscope, which combination of eyepiece and objective will give the least detail and the largest field of vision?

(*a*) 5*X* eyepiece, 10*X* objective

(*b*) 5*X* eyepiece, 44*X* objective
(*c*) 6*X* eyepiece, 10*X* objective
(*d*) 6*X* eyepiece, 40*X* objective.

Q. 1131. Which term includes the other three?

(*a*) digestion
(*b*) circulation
(*c*) metabolism
(*d*) synthesis.

Q. 1132. Animals may respond to a stimulus by secreting neurohumors and

(*a*) antibiotics
(*b*) hormones
(*c*) antigens
(*d*) mutagens.

Q. 1133. In humans, fats and carbohydrates are not directly converted into proteins because fat and carbohydrates lack

(*a*) carbon
(*b*) hydrogen
(*c*) oxygen
(*d*) nitrogen.

Q. 1134. Wastes are removed from the earthworm by

(*a*) nephrons
(*b*) nephridia
(*c*) Malpighian tubules
(*d*) contractile vacuoles.

Q. 1135. Which molecule contains the greatest amount of potential energy?

(*a*) glucose
(*b*) oxygen
(*c*) carbon dioxide
(*d*) lactic acid

Q. 1136. Atmospheric air contains approximately 0.04% carbon dioxide, whereas exhaled air may contain 4.5% to 5.0% carbon dioxide. Which process is most directly responsible for this difference?

(*a*) potosynthesis
(*b*) secretion
(*c*) hydrolysis
(*d*) respiration.

Q. 1137. Which organism is *least* dependent upon water for the excretion of nitrogenous wastes?

(*a*) hydra
(*b*) amoeba
(*c*) grasshopper
(*d*) man.

Q. 1138. In the hydra, the cells in the outer layer obtain nutrients directly from the cells in the inner layer by the process of

(*a*) diffusion
(*b*) excretion
(*c*) ingestion
(*d*) synthesis.

Q. 1139. In which organisms do *both* extra and intracellular digestion occur?

(*a*) in protozoans, only
(*b*) in algae, only
(*c*) in fungi but not in invertebrates
(*d*) in man but not in geranium plants.

Q. 1140. In humans, which is true of responses controlled by the nervous system?

(*a*) They are under the control of excretions from ribosomes
(*b*) They are associated with homeostasis
(*c*) They are slower than endocrine reactions
(*d*) They are not dependent upon the presence of ATP molecules.

Q. 1141. If the respiratory enzymes of an animal are destroyed, which process would most likely fail to occur in the cell membranes of that animal?

(*a*) osmosis
(*b*) diffusion

(*c*) molecular motion
(*d*) active transport.

Q. 1142. The function of the contractile vacuole is to

(*a*) exchange gases between the earthworm and its environment
(*b*) store most of the grasshopper's hydrolytic enzymes
(*c*) transmit impulses in a hydra's nerve net
(*d*) maintain water balance between a protozoan and its environment.

Q. 1143. In animal cells, amino acids are end products resulting from the digestion of

(*a*) lipids
(*b*) starches
(*c*) proteins
(*d*) fatty acids.

Q. 1144. Which animal does *not* have a specialized system for the transport of oxygen?

(*a*) grasshopper
(*b*) hydra
(*c*) earthworm
(*d*) man.

Q. 1145. The structure of the grasshopper's digestive system can best be compared to a

(*a*) sac
(*b*) spider's web
(*c*) tube
(*d*) bunch of grapes.

Q. 1146. Ammonia and energy are produced as a result of the chemical breakdown of molecules of

(*a*) simple sugars
(*b*) amino acids
(*c*) fatty acids
(*d*) glycerol.

Q. 1147. By which process is glycogen produced from glucose?

(*a*) oxidation
(*b*) hydrolysis
(*c*) dehydration synthesis
(*d*) fermentation.

Q. 1148. Most of the oxygen available to aerobic organisms results from the process of

(*a*) respiration
(*b*) chemosynthesis
(*c*) photosynthesis
(*d*) dehydration synthesis.

Q. 1149. Upon microscopic examination, cells treated with auxins would probably appear different from untreated control cells chiefly in their

(*a*) length
(*b*) color
(*c*) chromosome number
(*d*) cytoplasmic organelles.

Q. 1150. Animals which produce one or two egg cells during a singe reproductive cycle are most likely to have

(*a*) external fertilization and much parental care of the young
(*b*) external fertilization and little parental care of the young
(*c*) internal development and little parental care of the young
(*d*) internal fertilization and much parental care of the young.

Q. 1151. Which is formed during mitotic cell division in most plants but *not* in animals?

(*a*) nuclear membrane
(*b*) spindle apparatus
(*c*) cell furrow
(*d*) cell plate.

Q. 1152. In humans, the nucleus of which cell would contain the same amount of DNA as the nucleus of a somatic cell?

(*a*) mature egg
(*b*) polar body
(*c*) sperm
(*d*) zygote.

Q. 1153. Artificial parthenogenesis is the development of an egg cell which is

(*a*) fertilized after being treated with chemicals
(*b*) unfertilized but has been treated by chemical or physical means
(*c*) unfertilized and kept frozen until all enzymes are inactivated
(*d*) fertilized before being treated with chemicals.

Q. 1154. Which is an important biological advantage of sexual reproduction to a species?

(*a*) genetic variation in offspring
(*b*) production of more offspring
(*c*) production of larger offspring
(*d*) faster development of offspring.

Q. 1155. In vertebrates, genes are composed chiefly of

(*a*) DNA, only
(*b*) RNA, only
(*c*) DNA and RNA, only
(*d*) DNA, RNA and enzymes.

Q. 1156. In a double-stranded DNA molecule, the amount of cytosine is usually equal to the amount of

(*a*) uracil
(*b*) thymine
(*c*) guanine
(*d*) adenine.

Q. 1157. A man who has type AB blood marries a woman whose blood type is O. What are the chances that at least one of their children will be blood type B?

(*a*) 25%
(*b*) 50%
(*c*) 75%
(*d*) 100%.

Q. 1158. **If a child's father is colorblind and the mother has one gene for color blindness, what is the probability that the child may be colorblind?**

(*a*) 0%
(*b*) 25%
(*c*) 50%
(*d*) 100%.

Q. 1159. **In a cross between a homozygous dominant individual and a heterozygous dominant individual, the probability that an offspring will exhibit the recessive trait is**

(*a*) 0
(*b*) 1/8
(*c*) 1/4
(*d*) 1/2.

Q. 1160. **If the letter *T* represents the gene for the dominant trait, tall, and the letter *t* represents the gene for the recessive trait, short, which statement concerning the offspring is most likely correct if a cross is made betwen *Tt* and *Tt*? [Assume a large number of offspring.]**

(*a*) All of the offspring will be short
(*b*) All of the offspring will be tall
(*c*) Fifty percent of the offspring will be short
(*d*) Seventy-five percent of the offspring will be tall.

Q. 1161. **Segregation of hereditary factors occurs during the process of**

(*a*) fertilization
(*b*) succession
(*c*) recombination
(*d*) disjunction.

Q. 1162. **Which is an example of incomplete dominance?**

(*a*) Black and white guinea pigs, when mated, produce all black offspring
(*b*) Red short-horned cattle, when mated with white short-horned cattle, produce roan short-horned cattle
(*c*) Rough-haired guinea pigs, when mated, produce both rough-haired and smooth-haired offspring
(*d*) Tall pea plants with white flowers, when crossed with short pea plants with purple flowers, produce tall plants with purple flowers.

Q. 1163. Which is *not* normally a part of any nucleotide?

(*a*) deoxyribose
(*b*) thymine
(*c*) glycerol
(*d*) phosphate.

Q. 1164. Albinism in corn plants is caused by a recessive gene which prevents the plant from producing the chlorophyll essential for food production. Therefore, all albino plants in an F_2 generation die shortly after germinating. Nevertheless, albinos appear among members of the next generation because

(*a*) heterozygous green plants carry a gene for albinism
(*b*) homozygous green plants carry a gene for albinism
(*c*) only albinos are crossed
(*d*) heterozygous green plants are crossed with homozygous green plants.

Q. 1165. From the single-trait inheritance experiments, such as the tall X short cross of pea plants performed by Mendel, extensive data were collected that led him to conclude that

(*a*) the genotype of F_1 plants is the same as that of the parent plants
(*b*) chromosomes are carried by genes
(*c*) every plant has at least a pair of elements or factors for each trait
(*d*) the genotypes of all F_2 plants are identical to those of the parent plants.

Q. 1166. Which statement concerning evolution would most likely be attributed to Lamarck?

(*a*) organisms tend to produce more offspring than can survive
(*b*) The basis for variations in a species is provided by mutations
(*c*) Structures develop in organisms as a result of the organisms need to survive
(*d*) DNA replication is the key to evolution.

Q. 1167. All one-called organisms are classified as

(*a*) algae
(*b*) plants
(*c*) invertebrates
(*d*) protists.

Q. 1168. Many varieties of marsupials have evolved in Australia over a long period of time because of the

(*a*) geographic isolation of the continent
(*b*) internal development of the young marsupials
(*c*) coldblooded conditions of marsupials in a warm environment
(*d*) lack of deciduous tree on the continent.

Q. 1169. Darwin's theory of evolution made no attempt to explain

(*a*) the origin of life
(*b*) overproduction
(*c*) survival of the fittest
(*d*) natural selection.

Q. 1170. Evolution would probably occur most rapidly in population that is

(*a*) moderate in size and lives in a constant environment
(*b*) small and is subject to a high mutation rate
(*c*) large and is subject to a low mutation rate
(*d*) large and has become immune to natural selection.

Q. 1171. Body structures which are fundamentally alike and develop in the same way are

(*a*) embryological
(*b*) homologous
(*c*) heterozygous
(*d*) allelic.

Q. 1172. The scientific name for a cat is *Felis domestica*, and the scientific name for a lion is *Felis leo*. This indicates that the cat and the lion are in the same

(*a*) species, but in a different genus
(*b*) genus, but in a different species
(*c*) family, but in a different class
(*d*) species, but in a different family.

Q. 1173. "Earthworms live and reproduce in the soil. They aerate the soil and add organic material to it." These statements best describe an earthworm's

(*a*) habitat
(*b*) nutrition
(*c*) environment
(*d*) niche.

Q. 1174. All food chains in a community make up a

(*a*) hydrologic cycle
(*b*) food web
(*c*) world biome
(*d*) climax community.

Q. 1175. Malaria is caused by a protozoan that destroys red blood cells in humans. The relationship between humans and the protozoan is known as

(*a*) parasitism
(*b*) saprophytism
(*c*) mutualism
(*d*) commensalism.

Q. 1176. An ecosystem cannot continue functioning without a constant input of energy because

(*a*) energy is lost at each feeding level
(*b*) energy flow in an ecosystem is cyclic
(*c*) an ecosystem lacks organisms that store energy
(*d*) an ecosystem includes decomposers in its community.

Q. 1177. If the carbon dioxide content of the atomsphere were reduced, the first organisms to diminish in number would most likely be the

(*a*) producers
(*b*) primary consumers
(*c*) decomposers
(*d*) scavengers.

Q. 1178. Animals that eat both plants and animals are known as

(*a*) carnivores
(*b*) omnivores
(*c*) herbivores
(*d*) saprophytes.

Q. 1179. In humans, where is most digestion of carbohydrates and proteins completed?

(*a*) liver
(*b*) stomach
(*c*) small intestine
(*d*) midpoint of the large intestine.

Q. 1180. As a result of normal liver function, there is no prolonged increase in blood sugar after meals. This function contributes to the maintenance of

(*a*) homeostasis
(*b*) extracellular digestion
(*c*) assimilation
(*d*) inctracellular digestion.

Q. 1181. In humans, which structures join muscles to bones?

(*a*) tendons
(*b*) setae
(*c*) flexors
(*d*) ligaments.

Q. 1182. Most of the glucose in the blood of humans is transported by the

(*a*) red blood cells
(*b*) plasma
(*c*) platelets
(*d*) white blood cells.

Q. 1183. The human body adapts to living at high altitudes by producing

(*a*) more white blood cells
(*b*) more red blood cells
(*c*) fewer white blood cells
(*d*) fewer red blood cells.

Q. 1184. In which portion of the human alimentary canal does most water absorption occur?

(*a*) mouth
(*b*) stomach
(*c*) large intestine
(*d*) small intestine.

Q. 1185. In humans, which chamber of the heart does blood enter as it returns from the liver?

(*a*) lfet atrium
(*b*) left ventricle
(*c*) right atrium
(*d*) right ventricle.

Q. 1186. If a dog's pancreas were completely removed, what would be the effect on the concentration of glucose in its blood and urine?

(*a*) The glucose concentration would be normal in the blood and high in the urine
(*b*) The glucose concentration would be low in both the blood and the urine
(*c*) The glucose concentration would be high in the blood and low in the urine
(*d*) The glucose concentration would be high in both the blood and the urine.

Q. 1187. An injury to the cerebellum would most likely result in faulty

(*a*) memory
(*b*) hearing

(*c*) balance
(*d*) breathing.

Q. 1188. Which is *not* function of the liver?

(*a*) the production of insulin
(*b*) the breakdown of red blood cells
(*c*) the synthesis of glycogen
(*d*) the production of bile.

Q. 1189. Which is true of most of the carbon dioxide produced by a chicken embryo?

(*a*) It is not excreted
(*b*) It is destroyed by a chemical process
(*c*) It is released through the shell
(*d*) It combines with the yolk.

Q. 1190. Which group of animals stores the *least* amount of food in its eggs for its developing embryos?

(*a*) fish
(*b*) birds
(*c*) placental mammals
(*d*) nonplacental mammals.

Q. 1191. If fertilization is to occur, the human egg cell is normally fertilized within a short period of time after ovulation. During this time the egg will be

(*a*) undergoing meiosis in the ovary
(*b*) implanting itself in the ovary
(*c*) undergoing cleavage in the placenta
(*d*) moving through the oviduct.

Q. 1192. In humans, how many monoploid sperms would be produced in the gonads of the male from each primary sex cell?

(*a*) 1
(*b*) 2
(*c*) 8
(*d*) 4.

(A)

(B)

(C)

(D)

(E)

(F)

(G)

Diagram *A* represents the chromosomes in the nucleus of the somatic (body) cell of a worm. Diagrams *B* through *G* represent chromosomal arrangements which may occur in other cells produced by this worm.

Q. 1193. If meiosis failed to occur in both male and female worms, the zygote nucleus would resemble diagram

(*a*) *E*
(*b*) *G*
(*c*) *C*
(*d*) *D*.

Q. 1194. If crossing over occurred between a singe pair of homologous chromosomes during gamete formation, the gamete nucleus would most closely resemble diagram

(*a*) *F*
(*b*) *B*
(*c*) *C*
(*d*) *G*.

Q. 1195. The nucleus of a normal zygote formed when fertilization occurred in this species would most closely resemble diagram

(*a*) *E*
(*b*) *F*
(*c*) *C*
(*d*) *D*.

Q. 1196. The nucleus of a mature gamete from a female worm would most likely resemble diagram

(*a*) *E*
(*b*) *B*
(*c*) *C*
(*d*) *D*.

Q. 1197. The coded message of a messenger RNA molecule is believed to be determined by the

(*a*) amino acid sequence of an enzyme molecule
(*b*) base sequence of a DNA molecule
(*c*) monosaccharide sequence of a polysaccharide molecule
(*d*) fatty acid sequence of a lipid molecule.

Q. 1198. Between which types of compounds in a double-stranded DNA molecule must the bonds break before replication can take place?

(*a*) sugar–phosphate
(*b*) sugar–base
(*c*) purine base–pyrimidine base
(*d*) phosphate–base.

Q. 1199. The fact that DNA has been found in the chloroplasts and mitochondria of some cells is possible evidence of

(*a*) cytoplasmic as well as chromosomal inheritance
(*b*) bacterial transformation

(*c*) spontaneous mutations
(*d*) the presence of a mutagenic agent.

Q. 1200. Which is most probably the primary function of transfer RNA?

(*a*) to transport amino acids to messenger RNA
(*b*) to replicate the nucleotides of DNA
(*c*) to assemble molecules of nitrogen bases
(*d*) to shape the double helix of chromosomes.

Section XIII

Q. 1201. Which nitrogen base is *not* normally found in the DNA molecule?

(*a*) adenine
(*b*) uracil
(*c*) guanine
(*d*) thymine.

Q. 1202. The dissimilarities among living things are chiefly due to

(*a*) their physiological activities
(*b*) their DNA and RNA codes
(*c*) the type of bonding in their compounds
(*d*) the chemical elements in their protoplasm.

Q. 1203. One difference between a DNA nucleotide and an RNA necleotide is that the RNA nucleotide

(*a*) is found only in the nucleus
(*b*) is chemically more complex than a DNA nucleotide
(*c*) has more oxygen than a DNA nucleotide
(*d*) lacks a coding mechanism.

Q. 1204. Carries a hereditary code from the nucleus of a cell into the cytoplasm

(*a*) *A* and *C*
(*b*) *B*, only
(*c*) *C* only
(*d*) *B* and *C*.

DIRECTIONS (1204-1206): Each of statements 1204 through 1206 consists of a description. The diagrams below (A-C) are of nucleic acids. For each description, select from the diagrams below the nucleic acid or acids to which that description refers. In the space provided, write the number of the word or expression that best completes each statement or answers each question. (A number may be used more than once or not at all.)

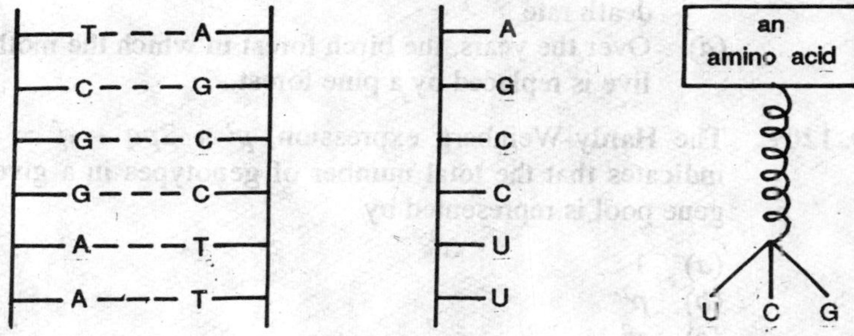

(A) (B) (C)

Q. 1205. Contains the original template that determines the individuality of an animal

(*a*) *A*, only
(*b*) *A* and *C*
(*c*) *C*, only
(*d*) *B* and *C*.

Q. 1206. Replicates itself during the processes of mitosis and meiosis

(*a*) *A*, only
(*b*) *B*, only
(*c*) *A* and *C*
(*d*) *B* and *C*.

Q. 1207. The appearance of a new bacterial strain characterized by its resistance to a particular antibiotic is most likely the result of

(*a*) gene mutation
(*b*) the inheritance of lethal genes
(*c*) the inheritance of acquired characteristics
(*d*) nonselective breeding.

Q. 1208. For a given species of moth, in which situation would the gene pool be msot likely to undergo change?

(*a*) No new species of moth enter the area, as every available niche is filled by the existing moth population
(*b*) Mating is random among moths of different shades of colour within the population
(*c*) The birth rate in the species becomes equal to the death rate
(*d*) Over the years, the birch forest in which the moths live is replaced by a pine forest.

Q. 1209. The Hardy-Weinberg expression, $p^2 + 2pq + q^2 = 1$, indicates that the total number of genotypes in a given gene pool is represented by

(*a*) 1
(*b*) p^2
(*c*) q^2
(*d*) $2pq$.

Q. 1210. Two organisms belong to the same species if they

(*a*) have the same chromosome number
(*b*) have the ability to produce the same antibodies
(*c*) can mate and produce fertile offspring
(*d*) go through a similar embryological development

Q. 1211. Which represents the most probable sequence of vertebrate evolution?

(*a*) fish –> reptiles –> amphibians –> birds
(*b*) fish –> amphibians –> reptiles –> birds
(*c*) amphibians –> reptiles –> fish –> birds
(*d*) amphibians –> fish –> reptiles –> birds.

Q. 1212. Which occurs as a result of adaptive radiation during the evolution of new animal species?

(*a*) No mutations appear.
(*b*) Available environmental niches are filled
(*c*) Natural selection ceases
(*d*) Random mating between species increases.

Q. 1213. In a certain population, which factor is the most probable cause of the change in the frequency of allele *y* as shown in the graph below?

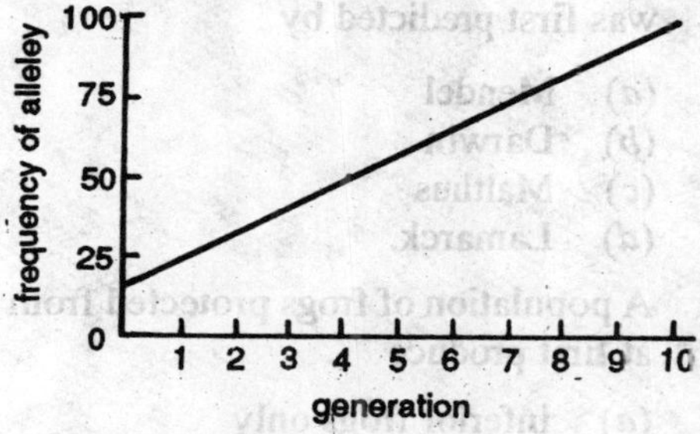

(*a*) selection in mating
(*b*) no migration of the members of the population
(*c*) a rapid increase in the size of population
(*d*) a constant environment.

Q. 1214. According to the heterotroph hypothesis, the earliest heterotrophs on earth carried on

(*a*) photosynthesis
(*b*) chemosynthesis
(*c*) anaerobic respiration
(*d*) aerobic respiration.

Q. 1215. Which condition does *not* contribute to gene pool stability?

(*a*) large populations
(*b*) random mating
(*c*) no mutations
(*d*) frequent migration.

Q. 1216. The fact that the Rh factor is found in the blood of rhesus monkeys as well as in human blood indicates that

(*a*) human blood is identical to monkey blood
(*b*) humans and monkeys may have a common ancestor
(*c*) humans descended from monkeys
(*d*) rhesus monkeys are related to humans but not to other monkeys.

Q. 1217. The total population of humans has risen at a rapid rate partly because of the removal of natural checks on population.

This has caused concern in many nations because the increase of human population has far outstripped the food-producing capacity of many ecosystems. This situation was first predicted by

(*a*) Mendel
(*b*) Darwin
(*c*) Malthus
(*d*) Lamarck.

Q. 1218. A population of frogs protected from all predation would at first produce

(*a*) inferior frogs only
(*b*) superior frogs, only
(*c*) smaller numbers of frogs
(*d*) greater numbers of frogs.

Q. 1219. A major physiological problem of marine-organisms is the

(*a*) tendency to lose excess salts from their tissues
(*b*) entrance of excess water into their tissues
(*c*) entrance of oxygen into their tissues
(*d*) tendency to lose body fluids from their tissues.

Q. 1220. Organisms that occupy similar niches in widely separated biomes are called ecological equivalents. Which pair represents ecological equivalents?

(*a*) wild horse and zebra
(*b*) seagull and codfish
(*c*) grasshopper and bean plant
(*d*) squirrel and rattlesnake.

Q. 1221. All organic compounds found in the biosphere contain

(*a*) ATP
(*b*) carbon
(*c*) nitrogen
(*d*) DNA.

Q. 1222. Which organic molecule is correctly paired with its simpler subunits?

(*a*) lipid–nitrogenous bases
(*b*) nucleic acid–inorganic bases

(*c*) carbohydrate–fatty acids
(*d*) protein–amino acids.

Q. 1223. Which cell structure is nonliving?

(*a*) endoplasmic reticulum
(*b*) chloroplast
(*c*) cell wall
(*d*) centrosome.

Q. 1224. A microscope has a 10 x eyepiece, and a 10 x and 40 x objective. The measured diameter of its low-power field is 1,200 microns. The diameter of its high-power field is

(*a*) 120 microns
(*b*) 12,000 microns
(*c*) 300 microns
(*d*) 400 microns.

Q. 1225. Which process does *not* directly involve the synthesis of chemical compounds?

(*a*) growth
(*b*) cell division
(*c*) reproduction
(*d*) egestion.

Q. 1226. Environmental factors which cause cells to move or to produce secretions are called

(*a*) stimuli
(*b*) synapses
(*c*) ganglia
(*d*) reflexes.

Q. 1227. In the Paramecium, which structure is the principal site of hydrolysis?

(*a*) food vacuole
(*b*) contractile vacuole
(*c*) analpore
(*d*) oral groove.

Q. 1228. Which organism contains a nerve net which enables impulses to travel in either direction?

(*a*) Hydra
(*b*) Amoeba
(*c*) Paramecium
(*d*) earthworm.

Q. 1229. Which structure is primarily involved in the transmission of impulses?

(*a*) platelet
(*b*) neuron
(*c*) vacuole
(*d*) nephron.

Q. 1230. To release the same amount of energy as an aerobe, an anaerobic organism would have to

(*a*) release more water
(*b*) absorb more oxygen
(*c*) oxidize more glucose
(*d*) use fewer enzyme molecules.

Q. 1231. The sequence of drawings (from left to right) is a simplified diagram representing a process which occurs in cells. What is the name associated with this process?

(*a*) simple diffusion
(*b*) passive transport
(*c*) pinocytosis
(*d*) osmosis.

Q. 1232. The selective transfer of particles through cell membranes is an important factor in the process of

(*a*) cytoplasmic streaming
(*b*) nuclear transfer

(*c*) homeostasis
(*d*) mechanical digestion.

Q. 1233. Which two organisms have closed transport systems?

(*a*) earthworm and human
(*b*) earthworm and protozoan
(*c*) grasshopper and human
(*d*) grasshopper and earthworm.

Q. 1234. During digestion, the principal function of water is

(*a*) act as a solvent for enzymes
(*b*) act as a medium for the storage of simple nutrient molecules
(*c*) dilute simple nutrient molecules and provide more surface area for enzyme action
(*d*) break down complex nutrient molecules by the process of hydrolysis.

Q. 1235. In aerobic respiration, oxygen functions as a

(*a*) carbon dioxide donor
(*b*) carbon dioxide acceptor
(*c*) hydrogen donor
(*d*) hydrogen acceptor.

Q. 1236. In which organism does digestion occur within a tube?

(*a*) Amoeba
(*b*) grasshopper
(*c*) protozoa
(*d*) Hydra.

Q. 1237. Locomotion in the earthworm is accomplished by the interaction of muscles and

(*a*) setae
(*b*) glands
(*c*) nephridia
(*d*) cartilaginous appendages.

Q. 1238. Nitrogenous wastes are most closely associated with

(*a*) base pairing
(*b*) dehydration synthesis

(*c*) protein metabolism
(*d*) carbohydrate metabolism.

Q. 1239. On which type of substrate are reactions catalyzed by lipases?

(*a*) fats
(*b*) proteins
(*c*) nucleic acids
(*d*) carbohydrates.

Q. 1240. Auxins are most closely associated with which process?

(*a*) evaporation
(*b*) root pressure
(*c*) regulation
(*d*) respiration.

Q. 1241. Animals do *not* possess enzyme systems which will permit their cells to make use of the energy in

(*a*) water
(*b*) carbohydrates
(*c*) fats
(*d*) proteins.

Q. 1242. Which organism's nervous system consists of a relatively simple anterior brain, a ventral nerve cord, and connecting nerves?

(*a*) mouse
(*b*) human
(*c*) frog
(*d*) grasshopper.

Q. 1243. Autotrophs differ from heterotrophs in that autotrophs

(*a*) utilize green light to synthesize food
(*b*) convert inorganic molecules
(*c*) possess adaptations for efficient locomotion
(*d*) do not require hydrolytic enzymes for digestion

Q. 1244. Which are formed during egg cell production in female mammals?

(*a*) zygotes
(*b*) spermatids
(*c*) spores
(*d*) polar bodies.

Q. 1245. For whcih combination is there the greatest need for the overproduction of egg cells so that the species may survive?

(*a*) internal fertilization and internal development
(*b*) internal fertilization and external development
(*c*) external fertilization and internal development
(*d*) external fertilization and external development.

Q. 1246. The ability to reproduce asexually is more often a characteristic of invertebrates than vertebrates because invertebrates

(*a*) possess more undifferentiated cells
(*b*) cannot produce gametes
(*c*) lack gonads
(*d*) undergo maturation and cleavage.

Q. 1247. A frog zygote begins to develop by a process known as

(*a*) meiotic division
(*b*) cleavage
(*c*) reduction division
(*d*) parthenogenesis.

Q. 1248. The structure pictured at the right is most closely associated with which process?

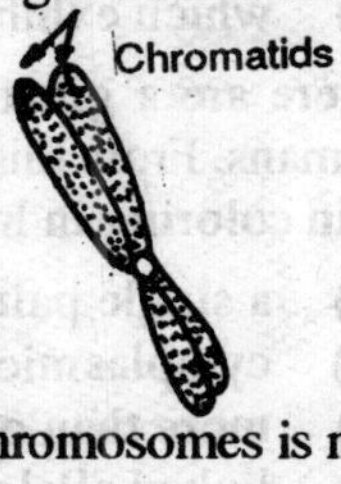

(*a*) mitosis
(*b*) cyclosis
(*c*) hydrolysis
(*d*) phagocytosis.

Q. 1249. The monoploid number of chromosomes is normally found in a

(*a*) flower petal
(*b*) fertilized sea urchin egg
(*c*) bean leaf
(*d*) mammalian gamete

Q. 1250. Normal mitotic division is a form of cell division in which the chromosome complement in each new cell is

(*a*) double the amount of that of the parent cell
(*b*) identical to that of the parent cell
(*c*) much different from that of the parent cell
(*d*) half the amount of that of the parent cell.

Q. 1251. If the genes for two different traits are located on the same autosome, the two traits would be expected to be

(*a*) inherited together
(*b*) visible in the offspring
(*c*) recessive in the offspring
(*d*) sex-linked

Q. 1252. With respect only to the alleles *G* and *g*, a heterozygous female could normally produce how many different kind of egg cells?

(*a*) 1
(*b*) 2
(*c*) 3
(*d*) 4.

Q. 1253. The relationship between heredity and environment can best be studied by using organisms

(*a*) with identical genotypes
(*b*) with a high mutation rate
(*c*) which are unrelated
(*d*) which exhibit polyploidy.

Q. 1254. There are a great number of shades of skin coloring in humans. From this fact, it may be assumed that the trait for skin coloring in humans is determined by

(*a*) a single pair of alleles
(*b*) cytoplasmic alleles
(*c*) more than one pair of alleles
(*d*) linked alleles.

Q. 1255. If heterozygous males with type *B* blood are crossed with heterozygous females with type *A* blood, what percent of their offspring can be expected to have type *O* blood?

(*a*) 25%
(*b*) 50%

(*c*) 75%
(*d*) 100%

Q. 1256. If a sperm cell in which nondisjunction of the sex chromosomes has occurred fertilizes a normal human female egg, how many chromosomes will the resulting zygote contain?

(*a*) 47
(*b*) 46
(*c*) 24
(*d*) 23.

Q. 1257. A hemophiliac man is married to a woman who has no genes for hemophilia. What is the probability that their first child will be a boy who is a hemophiliac?

(*a*) 0%
(*b*) 25%
(*c*) 50%
(*d*) 100%.

Q. 1258. When large numbers of roan cattle are interbred, percentages occur as following: 25% red, 50% roan, and 25% white. These results illustrate

(*a*) independent assortment
(*b*) blending inheritance
(*c*) dominance
(*d*) natural selection.

Q. 1259. The bony structure of a human's arm and hand most closely resembles the

(*a*) wing of a grasshopper
(*b*) wing of a butterfly
(*c*) wing of a bat
(*d*) fin of a shark.

Q. 1260. The modern horse has fewer toes than its ancestors. It is generally believed that such changes are governed by

(*a*) natural selection
(*b*) chromosomal deletions
(*c*) reduction division
(*d*) use and disuse.

Answer Sheet

Section I

1(*b*)	2(*b*)	3(*d*)	4(*b*)	5(*a*)	6(*c*)	7(*a*)	8(*d*)
9(*b*)	10(*b*)	11(*c*)	12(*c*)	13(*b*)	14(*d*)	15(*d*)	16(*d*)
17(*d*)	18(*c*)	19(*a*)	20(*c*)	21(*b*)	22(*c*)	23(*d*)	24(*a*)
25(*d*)	26(*a*)	27(*d*)	28(*b*)	29(*d*)	30(*c*)	31(*d*)	32(*a*)
33(*b*)	34(*c*)	35(*c*)	36(*a*)	37(*c*)	38(*d*)	39(*a*)	40(*b*)
41(*b*)	42(*c*)	43(*b*)	44(*c*)	45(*d*)	46(*d*)	47(*c*)	48(*b*)
49(*a*)	50(*b*)	51(*a*)	52(*b*)	53(*a*)	54(*a*)	55(*c*)	56(*d*)
57(*a*)	58(*c*)	59(*d*)	60(*c*)	61(*d*)	62(*a*)	63(*c*)	64(*c*)
65(*a*)	66(*d*)	67(*d*)	68(*b*)	69(*d*)	70(*a*)	71(*b*)	72(*d*)
73(*b*)	74(*c*)	75(*d*)	76(*d*)	77(*a*)	78(*c*)	79(*b*)	80(*d*)
81(*c*)	82(*d*)	83(*c*)	84(*d*)	85(*a*)	86(*b*)	87(*d*)	88(*d*)
89(*d*)	90(*c*)	91(*d*)	92(*a*)	93(*c*)	94(*d*)	95(*c*)	96(*d*)
97(*b*)	98(*b*)	99(*b*)	100(*c*).				

Section II

101(*b*)	102(*d*)	103(*c*)	104(*d*)	105(*a*)	106(*d*)	107(*b*)	108(*b*)
109(*a*)	110(*b*)	111(*c*)	112(*a*)	113(*b*)	114(*d*)	115(*b*)	116(*d*)
117(*b*)	118(*a*)	119(*a*)	120(*b*)	121(*a*)	122(*d*)	123(*c*)	124(*b*)
125(*b*)	126(*d*)	127(*c*)	128(*a*)	129(*d*)	130(*a*)	131(*c*)	132(*b*)
133(*b*)	134(*d*)	135(*d*)	136(*c*)	137(*d*)	138(*c*)	139(*c*)	140(*b*)
141(*a*)	142(*a*)	143(*a*)	144(*b*)	145(*b*)	146(*d*)	147(*a*)	148(*d*)
149(*a*)	150(*b*)	151(*b*)	152(*b*)	153(*d*)	154(*a*)	155(*a*)	156(*c*)
157(*c*)	158(*a*)	159(*c*)	160(*b*)	161(*a*)	162(*a*)	163(*b*)	164(*c*)
165(*c*)	166(*a*)	167(*a*)	168(*a*)	169(*c*)	170(*d*)	171(*b*)	172(*b*)
173(*d*)	174(*d*)	175(*d*)	176(*c*)	177(*b*)	178(*b*)	179(*d*)	180(*c*)
181(*b*)	182(*b*)	183(*a*)	184(*c*)	185(*c*)	186(*d*)	187(*b*)	188(*a*)
189(*d*)	190(*b*)	191(*d*)	192(*a*)	193(*b*)	194(*c*)	195(*a*)	196(*b*)
197(*a*)	198(*b*)	199(*b*)	200(*c*).				

Section III

201(*b*) 202(*d*) 203(*d*) 204(*a*) 205(*c*) 206(*c*) 207(*b*) 208(*a*)
209(*c*) 210(*c*) 211(*c*) 212(*a*) 213(*c*) 214(*d*) 215(*a*) 216(*b*)
217(*b*) 218(*a*) 219(*d*) 220(*c*) 221(*d*) 222(*a*) 223(*c*) 224(*d*)
225(*a*) 226(*c*) 227(*a*) 228(*b*) 229(*d*) 230(*c*) 231(*a*) 232(*a*)
233(*d*) 234(*d*) 235(*d*) 236(*d*) 237(*d*) 238(*b*) 239(*c*) 240(*a*)
241(*b*) 242(*a*) 243(*c*) 244(*c*) 245(*c*) 246(*a*) 247(*b*) 248(*b*)
249(*c*) 250(*a*) 251(*b*) 252(*b*) 253(*c*) 254(*b*) 255(*d*) 256(*c*)
257(*b*) 258(*b*) 259(*b*) 260(*a*) 261(*c*) 262(*d*) 263(*a*) 264(*d*)
265(*d*) 266(*c*) 267(*b*) 268(*b*) 269(*c*) 270(*b*) 271(*a*) 272(*a*)
273(*b*) 274(*d*) 275(*d*) 276(*b*) 277(*d*) 278(*d*) 279(*c*) 280(*d*)
281(*a*) 282(*c*) 283(*b*) 284(*a*) 285(*b*) 286(*d*) 287(*a*) 288(*c*)
289(*b*) 290(*d*) 291(*c*) 292(*c*) 293(*b*) 294(*a*) 295(*a*) 296(*c*)
297(*d*) 298(*a*) 299(*a*) 300(*c*).

Section IV

301(*a*) 302(*c*) 303(*b*) 304(*b*) 305(*c*) 306(*d*) 307(*a*) 308(*c*)
309(*c*) 310(*a*) 311(*d*) 312(*a*) 313(*b*) 314(*d*) 315(*a*) 316(*a*)
317(*c*) 318(*c*) 319(*d*) 320(*a*) 321(*c*) 322(*a*) 323(*a*) 324(*d*)
325(*c*) 326(*a*) 327(*b*) 328(*b*) 329(*d*) 330(*d*) 331(*c*) 332(*a*)
333(*a*) 334(*b*) 335(*b*) 336(*c*) 337(*b*) 338(*d*) 339(*b*) 340(*d*)
341(*a*) 342(*b*) 343(*d*) 344(*b*) 345(*c*) 346(*c*) 347(*c*) 348(*c*)
349(*b*) 350(*b*) 351(*b*) 352(*b*) 353(*d*) 354(*d*) 355(*b*) 356(*c*)
357(*d*) 358(*b*) 359(*c*) 360(*b*) 361(*a*) 362(*b*) 363(*c*) 364(*c*)
365(*a*) 366(*a*) 367(*d*) 368(*c*) 369(*b*) 370(*c*) 371(*b*) 372(*b*)
373(*a*) 374(*c*) 375(*c*) 376(*a*) 377(*c*) 378(*c*) 379(*d*) 380(*b*)
381(*c*) 382(*b*) 383(*b*) 384(*d*) 385(*c*) 386(*c*) 387(*c*) 388(*a*)
389(*c*) 390(*d*) 391(*a*) 392(*d*) 393(*d*) 394(*a*) 395(*c*) 396(*c*)
397(*b*) 398(*d*) 399(*d*) 400(*c*).

Section V

401(*b*) 402(*b*) 403(*a*) 404(*a*) 405(*b*) 406(*a*) 407(*d*) 408(*c*)
409(*c*) 410(*c*) 411(*d*) 412(*c*) 413(*b*) 414(*d*) 415(*a*) 416(*d*)
417(*a*) 418(*b*) 419(*a*) 420(*d*) 421(*b*) 422(*b*) 423(*a*) 424(*b*)
425(*d*) 426(*a*) 427(*a*) 428(*c*) 429(*a*) 430(*b*) 431(*a*) 432(*c*)

433(*d*) 434(*d*) 435(*a*) 436(*c*) 437(*c*) 438(*c*) 439(*c*) 440(*d*)
441(*c*) 442(*c*) 443(*d*) 444(*b*) 445(*c*) 446(*d*) 447(*c*) 448(*c*)
449(*b*) 450(*d*) 451(*a*) 452(*a*) 453(*a*) 454(*c*) 455(*c*) 456(*c*)
457(*d*) 458(*d*) 459(*b*) 460(*b*) 461(*b*) 462(*a*) 463(*d*) 464(*b*)
465(*d*) 466(*b*) 467(*b*) 468(*b*) 469(*c*) 470(*c*) 471(*d*) 472(*c*)
473(*d*) 474(*c*) 475(*c*) 476(*c*) 477(*c*) 478(*c*) 479(*d*) 480(*c*)
481(*d*) 482(*b*) 483(*b*) 484(*b*) 485(*d*) 486(*c*) 487(*b*) 488(*c*)
489(*c*) 490(*c*) 491(*c*) 492(*c*) 493(*c*) 494(*d*) 495(*b*) 496(*c*)
497(*c*) 498(*b*) 499(*b*) 500(*d*).

Section VI

501(*c*) 502(*c*) 503(*b*) 504(*a*) 505(*b*) 506(*d*) 507(*b*) 508(*b*)
509(*a*) 510(*b*) 511(*b*) 512(*a*) 513(*d*) 514(*d*) 515(*c*) 516(*d*)
517(*c*) 518(*c*) 519(*a*) 520(*d*) 521(*a*) 522(*c*) 523(*a*) 524(*c*)
525(*b*) 526(*a*) 527(*d*) 528(*b*) 529(*d*) 530(*c*) 531(*c*) 532(*d*)
533(*c*) 534(*d*) 535(*b*) 536(*c*) 537(*a*) 538(*a*) 539(*c*) 540(*a*)
541(*c*) 542(*a*) 543(*b*) 544(*d*) 545(*b*) 546(*a*) 547(*d*) 548(*b*)
549(*a*) 550(*c*) 551(*c*) 552(*d*) 553(*d*) 554(*a*) 555(*c*) 556(*c*)
557(*a*) 558(*c*) 559(*c*) 560(*c*) 561(*c*) 562(*a*) 563(*a*) 564(*c*)
565(*b*) 566(*c*) 567(*b*) 568(*a*) 569(*c*) 570(*b*) 571(*c*) 572(*c*)
573(*d*) 574(*b*) 575(*c*) 576(*c*) 577(*d*) 578(*b*) 579(*c*) 580(*a*)
581(*b*) 582(*b*) 583(*b*) 584(*d*) 585(*d*) 586(*d*) 587(*b*) 588(*b*)
589(*d*) 590(*a*) 591(*b*) 592(*d*) 593(*a*) 594(*a*) 595(*a*) 596(*b*)
597(*a*) 598(*b*) 599(*a*) 600(*d*).

Section VII

601(*b*) 602(*a*) 603(*c*) 604(*b*) 605(*c*) 606(*a*) 607(*c*) 608(*c*)
609(*d*) 610(*d*) 611(*b*) 612(*d*) 613(*a*) 614(*d*) 615(*c*) 616(*b*)
617(*b*) 618(*b*) 619(*b*) 620(*c*) 621(*c*) 622(*d*) 623(*b*) 624(*d*)
625(*a*) 626(*c*) 627(*b*) 628(*a*) 629(*b*) 630(*a*) 631(*d*) 632(*a*)
633(*b*) 634(*d*) 635(*d*) 636(*a*) 637(*d*) 638(*c*) 639(*a*) 640(*b*)
641(*a*) 642(*d*) 643(*c*) 644(*c*) 645(*a*) 646(*a*) 647(*c*) 648(*c*)
649(*c*) 650(*c*) 651(*d*) 652(*b*) 653(*d*) 654(*a*) 655(*d*) 656(*c*)
657(*c*) 658(*c*) 659(*c*) 660(*c*) 661(*b*) 662(*b*) 663(*d*) 664(*c*)
665(*a*) 666(*d*) 667(*b*) 668(*d*) 669(*c*) 670(*d*) 671(*a*) 672(*b*)

673(*c*) 674(*a*) 675(*c*) 676(*a*) 677(*b*) 678(*a*) 679(*d*) 680(*a*)
681(*c*) 682(*b*) 683(*c*) 684(*c*) 685(*d*) 686(*d*) 687(*d*) 688(*c*)
689(*b*) 690(*b*) 691(*c*) 692(*b*) 693(*c*) 694(*b*) 695(*c*) 696(*d*)
697(*d*) 698(*b*) 699(*d*) 700(*c*).

Section VIII

701(*d*) 702(*a*) 703(*a*) 704(*a*) 705(*a*) 706(*a*) 707(*a*) 708(*b*)
709(*d*) 710(*a*) 711(*b*) 712(*d*) 713(*a*) 714(*a*) 715(*b*) 716(*b*)
717(*d*) 718(*d*) 719(*b*) 720(*d*) 721(*b*) 722(*d*) 723(*b*) 724(*b*)
725(*a*) 726(*b*) 727(*c*) 728(*d*) 729(*b*) 730(*b*) 731(*b*) 732(*d*)
733(*c*) 734(*d*) 735(*d*) 736(*b*) 737(*b*) 738(*a*) 739(*b*) 740(*a*)
741(*b*) 742(*b*) 743(*a*) 744(*b*) 745(*a*) 746(*c*) 747(*b*) 748(*a*)
749(*a*) 750(*a*) 751(*a*) 752(*b*) 753(*c*) 754(*a*) 755(*b*) 756(*d*)
757(*a*) 758(*d*) 759(*c*) 760(*c*) 761(*c*) 762(*d*) 763(*b*) 764(*b*)
765(*b*) 766(*c*) 767(*d*) 768(*b*) 769(*a*) 770(*c*) 771(*d*) 772(*b*)
773(*d*) 774(*c*) 775(*d*) 776(*a*) 777(*b*) 778(*b*) 779(*d*) 780(*c*)
781(*b*) 782(*a*) 783(*a*) 784(*d*) 785(*b*) 786(*a*) 787(*c*) 788(*b*)
789(*c*) 790(*d*) 791(*d*) 792(*c*) 793(*c*) 794(*b*) 795(*b*) 796(*c*)
797(*a*) 798(*d*) 799(*b*) 800(*d*).

Section IX

801(*b*) 802(*a*) 803(*a*) 804(*a*) 805(*a*) 806(*c*) 807(*b*) 808(*c*)
809(*b*) 810(*b*) 811(*d*) 812(*c*) 813(*b*) 814(*b*) 815(*c*) 816(*a*)
817(*a*) 818(*a*) 819(*b*) 820(*c*) 821(*d*) 822(*a*) 823(*a*) 824(*b*)
825(*c*) 826(*a*) 827(*d*) 828(*a*) 829(*c*) 830(*d*) 831(*b*) 832(*d*)
833(*d*) 834(*a*) 835(*a*) 836(*d*) 837(*c*) 838(*a*) 839(*b*) 840(*d*)
841(*b*) 842(*c*) 843(*a*) 844(*d*) 845(*b*) 846(*b*) 847(*a*) 848(*a*)
849(*c*) 850(*b*) 851(*a*) 852(*b*) 853(*d*) 854(*b*) 855(*c*) 856(*a*)
857(*b*) 858(*d*) 859(*c*) 860(*b*) 861(*c*) 862(*d*) 863(*a*) 864(*a*)
865(*a*) 866(*c*) 867(*a*) 868(*d*) 869(*c*) 870(*a*) 871(*b*) 872(*d*)
873(*b*) 874(*d*) 875(*d*) 876(*b*) 877(*d*) 878(*b*) 879(*c*) 880(*d*)
881(*a*) 882(*c*) 883(*a*) 884(*d*) 885(*b*) 886(*b*) 887(*c*) 888(*a*)
889(*a*) 890(*d*) 891(*d*) 892(*c*) 893(*c*) 894(*b*) 895(*b*) 896(*a*)
897(*a*) 898(*c*) 899(*a*) 900(*b*).

Section X

901(*b*) 902(*b*) 903(*d*) 904(*c*) 905(*c*) 906(*a*) 907(*a*) 908(*c*)
909(*c*) 910(*c*) 911(*c*) 912(*c*) 913(*a*) 914(*d*) 915(*d*) 916(*b*)
917(*c*) 918(*b*) 919(*d*) 920(*d*) 921(*b*) 922(*c*) 923(*d*) 924(*c*)
925(*d*) 926(*c*) 927(*c*) 928(*b*) 929(*b*) 930(*a*) 931(*c*) 932(*a*)
933(*c*) 934(*a*) 935(*d*) 936(*c*) 937(*d*) 938(*d*) 939(*b*) 940(*c*)
941(*d*) 942(*a*) 943(*d*) 944(*c*) 945(*c*) 946(*b*) 947(*b*) 948(*d*)
949(*b*) 950(*a*) 951(*c*) 952(*c*) 953(*c*) 954(*c*) 955(*a*) 956(*c*)
957(*c*) 958(*c*) 959(*b*) 960(*c*) 961(*d*) 962(*c*) 963(*c*) 964(*b*)
965(*b*) 966(*d*) 967(*a*) 968(*a*) 969(*b*) 970(*a*) 971(*d*) 972(*a*)
973(*b*) 974(*c*) 975(*a*) 976(*a*) 977(*a*) 978(*d*) 979(*b*) 980(*b*)
981(*b*) 982(*c*) 983(*a*) 984(*c*) 985(*d*) 986(*a*) 987(*c*) 988(*a*)
989(*b*) 990(*a*) 991(*b*) 992(*d*) 993(*d*) 994(*c*) 995(*a*) 996(*d*)
997(*d*) 998(*d*) 999(*b*) 1000(*d*).

Section XI

1001(*a*) 1002(*a*) 1003(*a*) 1004(*b*) 1005(*d*) 1006(*a*) 1007(*a*)
1008(*a*) 1009(*b*) 1010(*d*) 1011(*d*) 1012(*d*) 1013(*b*) 1014(*d*)
1015(*c*) 1016(*d*) 1017(*c*) 1018(*b*) 1019(*a*) 1020(*c*) 1021(*d*)
1022(*b*) 1023(*a*) 1024(*c*) 1025(*a*) 1026(*b*) 1027(*c*) 1028(*b*)
1029(*c*) 1030(*b*) 1031(*a*) 1032(*b*) 1033(*b*) 1034(*c*) 1035(*d*)
1036(*c*) 1037(*b*) 1038(*c*) 1039(*c*) 1040(*d*) 1041(*d*) 1042(*c*)
1043(*c*) 1044(*a*) 1045(*a*) 1046(*a*) 1047(*c*) 1048(*a*) 1049(*c*)
1050(*d*) 1051(*b*) 1052(*a*) 1053(*c*) 1054(*b*) 1055(*d*) 1056(*b*)
1057(*a*) 1058(*d*) 1059(*a*) 1060(*a*) 1061(*c*) 1062(*d*) 1063(*c*)
1064(*c*) 1065(*d*) 1066(*a*) 1067(*d*) 1068(*c*) 1069(*d*) 1070(*c*)
1071(*c*) 1072(*d*) 1073(*b*) 1074(*a*) 1075(*b*) 1076(*c*) 1077(*c*)
1078(*d*) 1079(*a*) 1080(*c*) 1081(*c*) 1082(*d*) 1083(*c*) 1084(*b*)
1085(*b*) 1086(*a*) 1087(*d*) 1088(*c*) 1089(*d*) 1090(*d*) 1091(*b*)
1092(*a*) 1093(*d*) 1094(*b*) 1095(*d*) 1096(*c*) 1097(*a*) 1098(*d*)
1099(*d*) 1100(*c*).

Section XII

1101(*d*) 1102(*b*) 1103(*d*) 1104(*d*) 1105(*a*) 1106(*b*) 1107(*d*)
1108(*a*) 1109(*b*) 1110(*a*) 1111(*d*) 1112(*b*) 1113(*c*) 1114(*a*)
1115(*c*) 1116(*a*) 1117(*c*) 1118(*a*) 1119(*c*) 1120(*c*) 1121(*b*)

1122(*b*) 1123(*b*) 1124(*b*) 1125(*c*) 1126(*b*) 1127(*a*) 1128(*d*)
1129(*b*) 1130(*a*) 1131(*c*) 1132(*b*) 1133(*d*) 1134(*b*) 1135(*a*)
1136(*d*) 1137(*c*) 1138(*a*) 1139(*d*) 1140(*b*) 1141(*d*) 1142(*d*)
1143(*c*) 1144(*b*) 1145(*c*) 1146(*b*) 1147(*c*) 1148(*c*) 1149(*a*)
1150(*d*) 1151(*d*) 1152(*d*) 1153(*b*) 1154(*a*) 1155(*a*) 1156(*c*)
1157(*b*) 1158(*b*) 1159(*a*) 1160(*d*) 1161(*d*) 1162(*b*) 1163(*c*)
1164(*a*) 1165(*c*) 1166(*c*) 1167(*d*) 1168(*a*) 1169(*a*) 1170(*b*)
1171(*b*) 1172(*b*) 1173(*d*) 1174(*b*) 1175(*a*) 1176(*a*) 1177(*a*)
1178(*b*) 1179(*b*) 1180(*a*) 1181(*a*) 1182(*b*) 1183(*b*) 1184(*c*)
1185(*c*) 1186(*d*) 1187(*c*) 1188(*a*) 1189(*c*) 1190(*c*) 1191(*d*)
1192(*d*) 1193(*d*) 1194(*a*) 1195(*c*) 1196(*b*) 1197(*b*) 1198(*c*)
1199(*a*) 1200(*a*).

Section XIII

1201(*b*) 1202(*b*) 1203(*c*) 1204(*b*) 1205(*a*) 1206(*a*) 1207(*a*)
1208(*d*) 1209(*a*) 1210(*c*) 1211(*b*) 1212(*b*) 1213(*a*) 1214(*c*)
1215(*d*) 1216(*b*) 1217(*c*) 1218(*d*) 1219(*d*) 1220(*a*) 1221(*b*)
1222(*d*) 1223(*c*) 1224(*c*) 1225(*d*) 1226(*a*) 1227(*a*) 1228(*a*)
1229(*b*) 1230(*c*) 1231(*c*) 1232(*c*) 1233(*a*) 1234(*d*) 1235(*d*)
1236(*b*) 1237(*a*) 1238(*c*) 1239(*a*) 1240(*c*) 1241(*a*) 1242(*d*)
1243(*b*) 1244(*d*) 1245(*d*) 1246(*a*) 1247(*b*) 1248(*a*) 1249(*d*)
1250(*b*) 1251(*a*) 1252(*b*) 1253(*a*) 1254(*c*) 1255(*a*) 1256(*a*)
1257(*a*) 1258(*b*) 1259(*c*) 1260(*a*).